Jim Gary: His Life and Art

TOVA NAVARRA

HFN, Inc. Publisher
Brooklyn, New York

Jim Gary: His Life and Art

TOVA NAVARRA

Front cover: Diplodocus by Jim Gary. Photo by Tova
Navarra. Back cover: The author is pictured among Jim
Gary's Twentieth Century Dinosaurs, Hightstown, N.J.
Photo by Jim Gary.

Typography by Typographic Images, Inc., New York City

Printed in the United States by: Cosmos Communications

Contents

Acknowledgments i

Foreword
    I by Susan E. Stob ii
    II by Dennis M. Wint iii

Author's Note v

Introduction
    The Appeal of the Dinosaur 1

The Life and Art of Jim Gary 6

Catalogue of Works 52

Exhibitions 58

Collectors 62

Bibliography
    Published Sources on Gary 64

Photo Credits 82

About the Author 84

Acknowledgments

Max and Lillian Houss, patrons of the arts, deserve the foremost gratitude in the creation of this book. Artists throughout the centuries could not have made as historic and powerful a mark on the quality of our lives without those aesthetic souls who intensify the artists' efforts.

For his artistic insights and editorial eye, Louis de Furia is recognized and warmly appreciated.

Thanks also go to museum directors and staff members for their support of Jim Gary's sculpture exhibit, and to the editors, filmmakers and other artists who have recognized the scope of Jim's work and chosen to include it in theirs.

Foreword

I

An electric blue Dimetrodon, a forest green Apatosaur, and a shocking pink Pterosaur soaring in the fountain in Stanley Field Hall…the "Twentieth Century Dinosaurs" had arrived at the Field Museum of Natural History. To help celebrate the museum's annual Dinosaur Days in October, Jim Gary had been invited to display his Twentieth Century Dinosaurs in Stanley Field Hall, the main entrance hall. Before the invitation was extended many approvals had to be obtained. The administration had some reservations, but by now were used to the Education Department's unusual ideas and agreed to give us a free hand. With these details out of the way, the contract was signed and we all prepared for the arrival of the sculptures.

We greeted Jim Gary that sunny October day with great anticipation. I do not think any of us were prepared for the wonders that came off the flatbed truck. With Jim Gary's loving guidance, they all took on a feeling of life and vitality. As the preparators from Exhibition assisted Jim with installations of the sculptures, you could sense their excitement in the environment they were creating. Museum staff came from all over this enormous building to take part in this experience. In a single day Stanley Field Hall was transformed into a multicolored dinosaur habitat. All of this work was done with many museum visitors mingling around, getting more and more excited about the spectacle unfolding in front of their eyes.

How appropriate is an artist's showing of sculptures for a museum of natural history? A legitimate question that quickly faded once everyone saw the sculpture involved. The chairman of the Geology Department was impressed by the accuracy of the sculptures. On the other hand, Jim Gary spent a lot of time studying the fossil dinosaurs we have on display in our Dinosaur Hall. The accuracy of his sculptures did not come without many years of study. What better blend of art and natural history could we have?

The "Twentieth Century Dinosaurs" and Jim Gary did much to make Dinosaur Days 1984 a tremendous success at Field Museum. We were all very sad at the end of the month when we had to watch our wonderful dinosaurs being packed on the truck for the trip to their next temporary home. We all hope some will come back one day for a permanent stay. The importance of this wonderful display of colorful dinosaurs goes beyond the bright colors and fanciful groupings. They breathed life into the study of dinosaurs for all of our visitors. Dinosaur Days concentrated on the many interesting aspects of dinosaur study and the addition of Jim Gary's dinosaurs greatly enhanced this educational study.

Jim Gary, the artist, provided another dimension to the story. His personal involvement with his sculpture is obvious. The warmth of his personality and his genuine concern for the people he is working with make everyone feel at ease. From our plant person who spent two days collecting large plants from throughout the museum to enhance the space of the dinosaurs, to the Building Operations Manager, who went out of his way to have the Pterosaur installed in one of our fountains, all the Museum staff got involved in this project. Jim served as the catalyst for this unprecedented staff involvement. The museum visitor also benefited from his presence. Throughout Dinosaur Days he talked with visitors about his work and the dinosaurs they represented.

There is much more that could be said about Jim Gary and his work. These few words are just a sample of what has taken place in Jim Gary's life. He is a very special person and so is his sculpture. We look forward to his return to Field Museum.

Susan E. Stob
Department of Education
Field Museum
Chicago, Illinois
April 15, 1985

II

In 1979, while I was serving as director of the museum of the Academy of Natural Sciences of Philadelphia, Jim Gary came to meet with me about an exhibit of his sculptures. Because the museum had a natural history focus, my initial reaction was why would an artist be approaching a natural history museum with an art exhibit. Only a few minutes into the meeting, the answer was apparent. Jim Gary was no ordinary artist, but a visionary who took pieces of scrap metal, primarily from automobiles, and created the most fascinating dinosaurs one could imagine.

The sculptures were realistic representatives of the skeletal structures of dinosaurs. Jim would attach the approximate number of automobile brake shoes for the claws of the feet, leaf springs for the number of ribs, and lag bolts for the vertebral column.

The Academy was the first museum to host Jim Gary and his exhibit of dinosaurs, although Jim had previously exhibited at non-museum locations. When I first mentioned the possibility of an exhibit of metal dinosaurs, the reactions of the scientific staff ranged from skepticism to outrage. After all, Joseph Leidy, President of the Academy, described and named the first dinosaur ever discovered, and the Academy had a long and distinguished history in vertebrate paleontology dating from the 1850s.

The exhibit with about 20 of Jim's creatures opened in November 1979, and the public's response was overwhelming. The print and broadcast media picked up on the innovation and creativity of Jim and his creatures, and the visitors to the museum lined up to get in. Even the scientists enjoyed the exhibition and the attention it brought to the Academy.

During the several months of the exhibits and programs, I was able to get to know Jim and to appreciate him as an artist, teacher, and person. It takes a special vision to see something as unique and innovative in the junk parts of automobiles. Jim was not trained as an artist, but he has an internal skill and aptitude. He blends the skeletal structures of dinosaurs with the medium in a way no one had ever done before. As a teacher, Jim was able to inspire children in classes and programs by permitting them to create miniature versions of his dinosaurs, and the general visitor would watch and listen to him for hours as he demonstrated and explained his creations.

Dinosaurs are ''hot'' topics, interesting to both the scientist as well as the general public. Museums across the country have built new dinosaur halls and there are several touring dinosaur exhibits. Jim's dinosaurs were the first traveling exhibit in recent years and pre-dated the mechanical creatures as well as several scientific exhibits.

Through his creations, Jim has opened the eyes of people throughout the world to look at dinosaurs in a new way. I am very pleased that Jim will now be reaching people of all ages through this book, which illustrates so well his artistic skills as well as his outstanding person.

Dennis M. Wint
President
St. Louis Science Center
St. Louis, Mo.
January 1987

Author's Note

Viewers of art, being human, have a dogged sense of biology in their scrutiny of any structure to which a head, body and various append-ages can be attributed. From the magnified "bacillae" in the paintings of Miro to the ferociously *Homo sapiens* stances and emotions of bulls in Picasso's "Guernica," life forms register genus and species as we know them in their usual contexts.

In art, however, is the physical world stretched, warped, sliced, cubed, even obscured in deference to emotional impact. As we recog-nize Giacometti's linear man or Klee's birdy "Twittering Machine," so do we recognize in Jim Gary's sculptures a dinosaur, a flower, a woman, no matter how unorthodox the presentation by this artistic visionary. But viewers who eschew a provincial image and adopt a purely intellectual one have a chance to see design in the nude: ungar-nished free forms arguing mass versus delicacy, motion versus still life, and design within design.

Getting past the "Brontosaurus," for example, involves scanning its lines and planes as one would scan a poem for its meter. When its perforated volume is perceived at once as anchored and weightless, then can the viewer drop obvious prehistory in favor of the work's clunky rhythms to its tinklings. In addition, the sheer horizontal and vertical measure of the "Brontosaurus" as it looms over concrete or grass translates the "paper-doll-cutout" to a jarring effect. A viewer must step back for the parts' confluence, yet a tighter look shows how the character of each metal form not only articulates with its neigh-bors, but how deliberately varied spacing, like the columns of the Parthenon, appears correct *in toto* and inherits a sensual motion.

Gary's "skeletons" hoard an uncanny physical power unlike the frail, dusty bones of other creatures' remains; they thunder as they "walk"; they graze calmly, they flirt, they terrorize.

The "Allosaurus" is such a terror, though not as grand a presence as the "Brontosaurus." Instead, the "Allosaurus"' tense-curled tail and claws readied for the grasp reinforce a churlish expression with bared teeth. But as unpersonified design, the piece is reminiscent of a small explosion of mud, hefty, pointed splatterings that hang onto each other as they spread at gravity's pull. Even with the horizon are S-curves whipping the air (these are taken to the ultimate in Gary's fossil pieces that do not stand but lie on the ground—again, a drawing, or better, an assemblage). The legs are pedestal for the burst as it petrifies five feet above ground. The work is earthy as to be grainy dirt in balance and in anger provoked, perhaps, by an interloper.

The organic quality Gary worked into the "Allosaurus" is directly an opponent of the ethereal "Dimetrodon." From a slithery-footed base shoot tines sized so the tallest is in the middle of a bell curve. Head and tail relate to each other as those of tadpole form, but the work need not resemble a formidable lizard. Repeating a version of entasis in the projections animates the creature out of what might be frozen dentition and it moves playfully despite its futuristic silver and sleekness.

Gary's "Ant" is futuristic also, especially in size (six feet long) and facial expression. The piece is smooth and lacking any moist, clinging quality of real ants. Instead, it has power—the kind of power wrought of strong red, having majority over the primary-color scheme, a steadfast stance as opposed to live ants' constant motion, and the unexpected magnification of what is typically considered a repulsive form of life. Were it not an ant, it may simply be three segments with slender cylinders attached for adornment and contrast, or an aerial view of an island of red clay in thirds.

The rhythms of each sculpture bespeak Gary's multi-dimensional eye on the plane of Calder and Picasso. Both employed more than juxtaposed shapes: They unleashed relationships between caution and abandon. They sliced directly into intellect were it a hot bread, into senses were they butters. Gary pulls from metal its latent passions, anything from naiveté and sweetness to determination and cruelty. In short, Gary treats sculpture as biopsy, examining an entity's bits and nether aspects, then organizing them into a stunning, fluid whole. This is full-repertoire sculpture and mastery of the medium.

As one lifts stereotyped images from the sculpture, so can one remove Gary from the stereotyped artist to pioneer. The artworks, however engaging, are secondary to the spirit that produced them. The compulsions of explorers, inventors, philosophers, politicians, even famous entrepreneurs, are Gary's compulsions. He creates with foresight similar to knowing one can travel east to find the West before such route has been proven, and as though the Fountain of Youth is very much a valid destination. His innovations, particularly the engi-neering of his sculpture, bear the same characteristics as those of ancient Egyptian architecture, still studied in principle and artistry. As Renaissance sculpture reflected ancient ideals and updated the sensuality of art to the era, Gary's sculpture modernizes design, albeit recognizably prehistoric in the case of the dinosaurs, and connects with popular tastes while heating several eras into a fresh soup.

But Gary spent many years alone with his ideas. His works ventured into society with their "hulking charm," as one curator put it, as regularly as they could find a place. Even as each place became spotlight, for overwhelming attention was paid to the pieces, Gary persisted in his larger-than-art concepts. He felt the tremors caused by his "Universal Woman," also known as the "Washer Woman," as he embarked on a career as an artist. He sensed the vitality of his "Stained Glass Lady" and of his pioneering use of stained glass in three-dimensional sculpture. This piece harvests physical and metaphorical tensions of all Gary's sculptural devices.

That Gary produced an exhibit of permanent value and appeal—a series of works which communicates readily to all levels of perception—and is consistently able to take it to museums has set a precedent for other modern artists with fresh ideas. Rarely, if ever before, has an individual artist unrepresented by gallery or agent been so successful as to be in demand. And rarely, if ever, has an artist been able to earn a living by rutting international paths with the wheels of a flat-bed trailer carrying weighty and provocative works of art.

As the sculptor tends the fibers between him and the business of his work, he must preen the works, sophisticate and polish them. Their transitions through the years are evident. Gary's "Tyrannosaurus rex" sculptures, among other examples, began with boxier, emphatically segmented forms. They have evolved, as it were, into confident sculptures that stalk the terrain of imagination. The viewer has the option of his own aesthetics thereafter to judge what the sculpture represents.

Gary's latest works hold an inimitable internal rhyme. Birds, butterflies, dinosaurs, torsos—if we insist upon organic classification—wallow in subtle gradations of luminosity and tone, a celebration of metal as it dances in the fire. Detail photographs of any of Gary's sculptures result in compelling, painterly abstracts. They are studies in composition, color (at times as Mondrian conjured "White on White" for the formerly indiscriminating glance), and motion. No martinets, these works. Gary has set out to detain the viewer's eye as often as to amuse it and let it play from whatever vantage the viewer prefers.

And at last, let us remove the presumptuous lay status of most viewers, and watch erudite respondents emerge, applauding the parcels of Gary's artistic wisdom that touch and court them.

Introduction

The Appeal of the Dinosaur

"We cannot trap them in our zoos, oh, no!
They seem to haunt us everywhere we go...
they wedge between our actions and our dreams
and throw their shadows on our movie screens...
...they are our steady progress and the lack of it."

So wrote Carolyn Stoloff in her poem "Dinosaurs." Her images are straightforward: Dinosaurs represent an extinction that may befall man himself, though extinctions within man's history, his omissions, wastes and oversights, are already clear. The sculptor in Jim Gary has produced a material litany to these extinctions. Dinosaurs are his art, his fantasy and his career, and the making of them as sculpture depends upon discards of, yes, extinct automobiles.

While Gary's work brought dinosaurs to the fore of the art world, let us examine how dinosaur themes have enjoyed irrepressible popularity as the focus of both art and science.

Deinos, or *dinos*, means terrible.

Sauros means lizard.

Together the two Greek words describe one of the most fascinating groups of animals that ever roamed the earth. As a science, the study of dinosaurs thrives on discoveries of fossils, bones, even dinosaur eggs which, when scanned under computerized tomography, show dinosaur embryos. Scientists continue to dispute whether dinosaurs were warm-blooded mammals or cold-blooded reptiles, and whether it was an asteroid or comet storm or a great shift in the earth's environment that put an end to more than 140 million years of their existence.

Robert T. Bakker, adjunct curator at the University of Colorado Museum in Boulder, says dinosaurs were more like birds and mammals, who could forage and dominate large areas and other species in order to survive. His book "The Dinosaur Heresies: New Theories Unlocking the Mystery of the Dinosaurs and Their Extinction," published by William Morrow & Co. in 1986, is testimony to the freshness of the debate and wonderment over dinosaurs.

Perhaps those who pursue careers as paleontologists or in related fields involving the study of dinosaurs follow a childhood fascination into adulthood. Harvard biologist Stephen Jay Gould wrote in The New York Times Book Review, Oct. 19, 1986, that he is still in his dinosaur phase!

"I knew exactly what I wanted to do as an adult. I would study dinosaurs, a firm conviction inspired by one supreme moment of childhood terror dissipated by fascination—my first look at Tyrannosaurus rex in the American Museum of Natural History."

Gould's colleague, psychologist Sheldon White, maintains that a passion for dinosaurs may be attributed to their being "big, fierce and extinct." But Gould said these characteristics "are not the stuff of permanent commitment. The Empire State Building is big, and Rambo is both fierce and ought to be extinct. The promotion of dinosaur mania to a career demands a matrix of ideas to absorb and channel that primal phenomenological oomph."

The "oomph" takes many forms, and our museums and media provide them. The first thing every child wants to see in a museum is the dinosaurs, says Amy J. Wolff, who worked at the Harvard Museum of Comparative Zoology before she opened the Dino Store in Cambridge, Mass., in the fall of 1986. "The tiniest kids, kids that can barely say their own names, can say brontosaurus," Wolff said in a front-page New York Times article on Oct. 21, 1986. The Dino Store is "an entire emporium devoted to the reptilian paraphernalia of kiddie culture," according to Gould.

Department stores including Bloomingdale's and Macy's have used dinosaur themes. The sale of dinosaur toys, T-shirts, neckties, books, bed linens, cookware, banks, puppets, kites, stationery and Halloween costumes, to name a few items, has become the rage. From F.A.O. Schwartz's "Toys of Extinction" boutique to Macy's "34,000 B.C." dinosaur shop, dinosaurs emerge not only as big and fierce, but as cute and lovable.

Some media dinosaurs are so cute and lovable, in fact, that people want to adopt them more than they want to conquer them. (Either is pure fantasy: Dinosaurs were long extinct before man came to be.) The film "Baby," a 1985 Disney production, portrays a baby brontosaurus whose fetal look and newborn innocence bring forth anyone's maternal instinct, even though the movie itself may not represent anything more than dinosaur memorabilia in years to come. "Dino,"

the household pet of television's cartoon family, "The Flintstones," was about the size of a baby elephant and had both sweet and spiteful traits attributable to any pet.

The dinosaur image used as a trademark of yesteryear's Sinclair gasoline stations—a bright green brontosaurus—also softened "big and fierce" into enduring and powerful. But people relish "Godzilla," the mean Tyrannosaurus, and "Rodan," a terrorizing pteradactyl, both of Japanese film fame, as much as they are charmed by endearing versions of the species. King Kong, an American anti-hero, wrestles a Tyrannosaurus to its death as an act of love for his woman, played by Fay Wray. The movie "Caveman," starring Ringo Starr in CBS-Fox's 1981 production, pits man against the carnivorous monsters. And the Loch Ness monster of Scotland, which some claim is a living Plesiosaurus, is pursued relentlessly by those infected by the dinosaur bug.

A fearsome Tyrannosaurus appeared on the cover of Time magazine's May 6, 1985 issue. The colorful drawing by Braldt Bralds was certain to attract attention and buyers who would read about the latest theories on why the dinosaurs lost their reign. Some of those readers may have been fans of the comic strip "Alley Oop," a caveman who seemed to live peaceably among the dinosaurs, or those who would find Dinamation dinosaurs (fleshed-out models that move their heads from side to side) engaging. And many of them would purchase stuffed dinosaurs or model kits for their children (so they say). Dinosaurophiles are an ageless crowd.

"Perhaps there is a little Jim Gary in us all," wrote Bob Cerullo in AutoWeek, Feb. 7, 1983, "secretly motivating us to save all sorts of old parts in dark corners of the garage to form someday the parts of our own creatures." Gary himself, who often calls his sculpture "Detroit dinosaurs," visits auto salvage yards the way an archeologist goes on a dig, in search of parts that would correspond with the designs in his mind. "But of all the odd pieces of bric-a-brac made from various bits and pieces of cars, none can compare with the truly incredible work of…Jim Gary. Gary is a sculptor whose chisel is a welding torch, whose quarry is an automobile junkyard and whose imagination is as immense as the creatures he creates…. His massive works are frighteningly realistic as well as ingenious—aside from being a perfect way to use up old automobile parts," wrote Cerullo, a leading columnist in the mechanics field. Gary's ability as an artist and historian has been praised by editors, art critics, writers, teachers and scientists.

An editorial entitled "Tyrannosaurus wrecks" in the Pittsburgh Post-Gazette, April 20, 1982, offered this insight: "Quite aside from the artistic merit of the replicas, it's remarkable that Mr. Gary was able to find in junkyard wrecks the levers, gears and panels so imitative of the bones, joints, teeth and armor-plate of those fascinating beasts—Tyrannosaurus rex and the rest—which lived millions of years ago.

"Moreover, the museum (Carnegie Institute) ingeniously held a 'Junkosaurus' contest (conceived by Gary and initiated in many museums in conjunction with his show) for schoolchildren from kindergarten through the eighth grade to make dinosaurs and other ferocious animals out of waste materials. Everybody but an old fossil would enjoy the varied results."

The writer of the editorial also pointed out that Gary's sculptures were displayed under the same roof with the renowned Carnegie dinosaur collection, "one of Pittsburgh's prime attractions for most of this century…. All told, 'Twentieth Century Dinosaurs' is one of the cleverest combinations of fun and learning to occur in Pittsburgh in some time."

Hundreds of other articles about Jim Gary's work reiterate the public's craving for dinosaur exhibits. The Boston Museum of Science, which displayed Gary's dinosaurs for four months, said it best with the title of its dinosaur show: Romancing the Dinosaur. Indeed, Gary's art is a romance, linking the elements of the Old Masters with elements of science, history and technology.

The Life and Art of Jim Gary

For Jim Gary, privacy has long been a frustrating issue, as it has with many artists.

Post-Impressionist Paul Gauguin left Paris, his family and his prosperity as a stockbroker to spend his life as an artist in Tahiti. His desire was for a privacy of environment, a place away from everything he'd known before and where his eyes would become "new" eyes upon a "primitive" world. Michelangelo seemed at odds with the world, and Georges Seurat, a pointillist, has been portrayed recently in the Broadway play "Sunday in the Park with George" as totally absorbed by himself and his art. Paul Cézanne lived in isolation, painting landscapes and still lifes. The list goes on.

Artists often seek intense forms of privacy—escape, if you will—yet they want to show and sell their work to as many people as possible. And as the work, paintings or sculpture, reveals to viewers an artist's most intimate moments, thought and visions, so do artists lie vulnerable to the viewer's welcome, indifference or rejection. Privacy may be reduced to a mere illusion, then, as an entire life unfolds in the art form, naked to the "voyeurs" the artists pray will become multitudes.

Such artistic intimacies placed in the public eye are not only subject to viewing by the layman, but to analysis by art historians and critics, who have the potential to educate the public, to argue persuasively that an artist's work is either dispensable or noteworthy.

Once past the critical lions, the work must deepen and expand if it is to become a cornerstone of style and artistic philosophy. Ultimately, no matter what comedy or tragedy the work represents, it must make people happy to have seen it.

"The day will come," Pablo Picasso said, "when the sight of a painting will ease the pain of a toothache." His statement marks his profound comfort and truth in art, which, despite invasions by the public eye, lives its own private life.

From this vantage, chronicling Jim Gary's life and work takes on a Rousseauan mythological aspect. Not every artist feels obligated to write his personal manifesto, or even to document his work in a formal manner, and Jim Gary is one. His art, he said, "stands alone. Nothing more is required from the artist but the art."

Upon this foundation, Gary produces a range of metal sculptures that tell all that Gary wishes viewers to know; when they do not grasp his point but choose to see another, he is tolerant and amused. When they ask not how and why the sculpture came into the material world, but who and of what extraction is the artist, Gary recoils into an impenetrable armor.

The artworks do provide a code for Gary's tumultuous, private messages, though in his career as a sculptor for the past fifteen years, he has managed to distract reporters, filmmakers, and others probing into his life beyond art with the fact that his sculpture is emotional.

The media are romanced not by the circumstances of his childhood or the "against-the-odds" success of a black artist, which Gary refuses to even think about, but by a variety of art unlike any other.

However elusive his speech, Gary's wit and wisdom find their way into each piece, dinosaur, bird, abstract or nude.

Gary's "Universal Woman" is a case in point. Five feet of femininity transcend a humble birth from cold metal washers welded together. Dissatisfied, Gary put the work aside for a time. Then he was invited to show his work in the National Black Artists Exhibition, sponsored by the Smith-Mason Gallery of Art, in Washington, D.C., in 1971. As was his desire for each art exhibit, Gary wanted to show a new piece.

The torso of the "Universal Woman," headless, forearmless, footless, reminiscent of "Nike of Samothrace" and "Venus de Milo," was dredged from among other works in progress. Hundreds of ordinary automotive washers offered an exquisite frontal nude. Curves about the shoulders and breasts and the "flesh" betraying sensual hints of the pelvic girdle were no less desirable and realistic than Pygmalion's Galatea in full proportion. A product of nearly undetectable welding, the washers were transformed into lacy body-cell clusters, poised for dancing.

After deciding to show the piece under the auspicious premise that less is more, Gary won the James V. Herring Award (Herring was a professor emeritus of Howard University) for sculpture—$500—for it. Clearly, it is finished; the addition of one more washer would allow a viewer to reach less vigorously for physiological closure and aesthetic emphasis.

In a subsequent sidewalk art show in Sea Bright, on the coast of New Jersey, the "Universal Woman" gathered ribbons and prize money for its irony and classicism. A man in khaki pants and a plaid shirt wandering through the show approached Gary and his "Universal Woman."

"I wish I'd thought of it," the man said. Then he criticized the pedestal on which Gary had placed the work as not what the sculpture deserved, that a marble or other, sleeker base would enhance it.

"I know what I'm talking about," the man said. "I'm a stonecutter. Look me up in an art book." He told Gary his name: Jacques Lipchitz. Lipchitz died the following year, 1973, at the age of 82.

Eventually, Gary did change the pedestal as Lipchitz had suggested, and an unforgettable suggestion it was. Had it not come from a noted artist, Gary may never have altered his stubbornness about his work that is synonymous with surviving an artist's life. Gary believes it is the work itself that must shine through the dullest of surroundings.

Gary is living testimony to this tenet, for he was the only one of eleven siblings who was creative, ambitious, and fiercely independent. Born in Florida on St. Patrick's Day, 1939, and brought immediately thereafter to New Jersey by parents who wished to avoid racial discrimination in the South, Gary spent his childhood in Colts Neck Township.

Charles and Lula Belle Gary settled in a seven-room ranch on a rural piece of land on Muhlenbrink Road in Colts Neck, between Freehold and Red Bank. There they were able to grow vegetables and raise cows, pigs, and chickens to round out the family's food supply. Jim shared a room with one of his brothers. During winter months, the two boys took turns staying up all night to keep aglow their source of heat—a wood-burning stove. Of all the rooms in the drab house, Jim liked the kitchen best, "where the food was," he said as he recalled his mother's seven-layer chocolate cake, a treat that came far too seldom to the Garys. They were one of two black families in Colts Neck in the 1940s, and ekeing out a living meant that all the children who could walk had to work.

Charles Gary, a farmhand and a mason of some artistic note in Jim Gary's gimlet child's eye, kept his children busy with chores "from sunup to sundown," said Gary, "even if the job was blowing straw into the wind." Because tending the livestock and the garden dominated Gary's early years, Gary decided then and there that his life's work would resemble as closely as possible the play he desperately missed. By the age of eleven, Gary had established a desire to work outside his family's territory. On the other side of Colts Neck lived the Sterners, a prominent, wealthy family that usually employed live-in help. Gary persuaded E. Donald Sterner to hire him to rake leaves and do odd jobs. If Gary earned 50 cents, his father took all but a nickel, which Gary spent on bubblegum or something that would last as long or longer.

Gary was unhappy that his earnings were confiscated. He was embarrassed to wear hand-me-down clothes to school where his classmates recognized the clothing they had outgrown and donated to poor families. One day he told his mother, a domestic when she could find work, that he wanted to get an early start the next day at the Sterners' and that he was going to spend the night there. She consented, probably relieved that there would be one less mouth to feed. Gary edited the fact that the Sterners did not know of his plans to sleep in their garage, though there he slept undiscovered time after time.

The morning he overslept put an end to his caper, for Dorothy Sterner opened the garage door to find the little boy who worked for her and her husband.

"How long have you been staying here like this?" she asked.

"A year," came the boy's reply.

With that, Mrs. Sterner provided Gary a room in the cellar of the large house, a room he did not have to share. She bought him new clothes and fed him three meals a day as long as he wished to work for them.

Her kitchen, Gary remembers, was immaculate and well-equipped with copper pots and modern appliances. It was a generous kitchen in which he learned to cook so well that later, the Sterners urged him to become a chef. Mrs. Sterner even tried to help him with his homework, which did not entice him as much as the bicycle he made for himself from scavenged pieces or the go-cart he constructed for his innate love of moving fast.

During his years at Freehold High School, Gary's creations in woodshop class won him prizes and special encouragement of the teacher. He was co-captain of the gymnastics team but eschewed his grammar-school nickname, "Tiny Tim," because he was tall and slender. But Gary's art teacher gave him a failing grade for the green rabbits and other odd color schemes that, she could not have predicted, were to evolve into a green Brontosaurus, a silver Dimetrodon, and a burgundy Tyrannosaurus rex that today charm museum visitors all over the world.

After high school, Gary joined the Navy, where military regimentation continued his father's seemingly inexhaustible demands. "You could do a thing one of three ways: the right way, the wrong way, or the Navy way," Gary said wryly. "I used to get up and finish a task long before my father got up in the morning, just to avoid having to do something *his* way."

In the Navy, Gary earned an aviation mechanic's license. He knew aircraft engines inside out. Upon his return to civilian life, Gary took a job at Lakehurst (N.J.) Naval Engineering Center prepared to use his expertise. But he was relegated to sweeping the hangar and doing minor repairs on a tractor. After several months, Gary had had enough.

He got a job pumping gas at a gas station in Colts Neck. The Sterners were appalled. They did not realize that Gary had applied for and was awaiting a position as a Job Corps staff member, which materialized in about five months. But the incoming Nixon administration terminated the entire Job Corps, in which Gary served for three years as a processor of Job Corps trainees.

"It's the one thing I can thank President Nixon for," Gary quipped years later, for leaving the Job Corps spurred him into devoting all his time to art. The unemployment agency couldn't find him a comparable job as an alternative, and offered working in stockyards, for instance. Somehow, Gary felt destined for a more exciting life, and soon his art gallery in Colts Neck was born.

The gallery served as showplace, but most of the work processes actually took place in a former chicken coop in Howell Township Gary rented from the farmers Bienstock, Joseph and his son Marshall. Gary paid part of the electric bill and an additional small amount for about a third of a 30' x 50' shop, which he shared with Marshall Bienstock, plus room outdoors for the gigantic sculptures Gary was making at the time.

"He put in a lot of hours, depending on his projects," said Marshall Bienstock. "My sister Elsa was Jim's assistant for a while, and it was she who initiated his renting workspace here. My workshop door was on national TV and the subject of stories by many reporters when Jim was here!" Bienstock said much of Gary's work influenced him, and that Gary taught him how to weld the farm machinery he worked on.

"I'm a practical welder, not an artistic one," Bienstock said. "But I was impressed and bemused by Jim's work—he's definitely a creative person.

"We had a sort of antagonistic relationship, which is probably why Jim eventually left. (He was here from 1969 to 1980.) We were similar—stubborn and a little paranoid. When you work side by side, you tend to get on each other's nerves. But we were always straightforward with each other. Jim's a very decent person and he is driven by success and strong will," said Bienstock.

Gary often worked so long and hard in Howell that he depended upon Carol East, then of Middletown Township, to run the gallery in Colts Neck.

"The Iron Butterfly Gallery was a wonderful old rustic building with a fireplace where really nice art shows and open houses were held," said Mrs. East, who now resides in Birmingham, Alabama. "When I met Jim at one of the gallery's wine-and-cheese parties for a local club—I was a club member and in charge of the party—I was impressed by the quality and quantity of his work. I ended up running the gallery for four years until I moved to Alabama.

"When Jim is in the process of creating, he's not interested in anything else. Something would come up at the gallery that I felt I couldn't handle, and Jim would say, 'You take care of it, Carol.' Jim was liberal with me and very supportive; I pretty much could make the decisions, doing what I thought was best," she said.

"There were times, though, when Jim wanted instant results. He is impatient. We argued an awful lot (I can be hard-headed also); he was always running late and I always yelled about that. I'd be frantic at some of the gallery openings, because fifteen minutes before people were to arrive, Jim would still be welding a piece.

"But for some reason, he trusted me, and it was like having a baby—when the baby is three months old, you've forgotten about all the screaming and yelling."

Gary says Mrs. East, "bar none, was the best gallery director I've ever worked with. She was innovative and willing to reach out to the community. I'm still asking her when she's coming back."

Mrs. East expresses as undaunted an appreciation of Gary's sculpture as of him as a friend. "If hours could make success, Jim would be the greatest, Bogie (her husband William) always said. We knew him when he worked night and day and was just starting out, and we were delighted when he began to be discovered," Mrs. East said.

One of the first major glories was Gary's winning the top honor for the "Universal Woman," for which Mrs. East posed. He worked painstakingly on the torso, "turning unpliable nuts and bolts into soft curves—I'm thrilled with it," she said. She is also proud of other sculptures by Gary in her collection.

"I had taken some old, odd pieces from my grandfather's farm, you know, as a keepsake. They were various pieces of plows and other things, some practically unidentifiable. Jim took them, and one night, around midnight, he called and said he was on his way over.

"When he got here, he set down a duck made of the pieces—a duck with a spring neck that moved. He has such a wonderful imagination. He sees things in nothing."

The Easts' coffee table by Gary is a 5' x 2½' "stainless steel base, a glass top, and everything in the world in it," Mrs. East said, "pliers, a wrench, gears, nuts, bolts, screws. It's a marvelous conversation piece."

A 10-foot tall, blue and orange abstract Gary had given them as a housewarming gift stood in the Easts' yard until it was demolished by a tree blown over during a storm. He'd since gone back to his shop and created another piece—exactly the right abstract sculpture to fit under their cathedral ceiling. Gary is prolific as he is sensitive to space, as zealous a worker as he is an artist.

Toward the latter half of the eleven years Gary maintained his shop with the Bienstocks, major recognition for his work began to surface and museum shows were on the horizon. In fact, it was not long after his Philadelphia Academy debut that Gary's Red Bank Studio was open to the artistic community, and his workshop went from Howell to Hightstown.

On March 11, 1979 a fire gutted the building that housed Gary's second-floor studio. Many of the artworks, as well as awards, scrapbooks and other records of his blossoming career, were destroyed. According to the Asbury Park Press report on March 12, the cause of the fire—and its subsequent smoke and water damage—may have been an electrical fault somewhere in the tobacco store on the ground level. An estimated 125 men fought the blaze.

Now Gary had no place to stay until the heat, electrical supply and water were restored and the fire damage cleared and patched. His new publicity agent and assistant, Arlene Berg, offered him either a large room with a private bath in the cabana or a room in her Oceanport home, where she lived with what she called her "one-TV family." Gary chose the room in the house.

"Watching television and movies is basically how Jim relaxes around the weird hours he works," Mrs. Berg said. "My three children enjoyed having him around—he was a new person in the household. For myself, there was a bit of additional pressure always having someone in the house, but it was never a nuisance. Jim liked to cook and always cleaned up afterward—he didn't add commotion."

About six months after Gary's studio was made livable again, a faulty boiler caused a powerful jet of steam to repeat the damage. Until that was repaired, Gary was thankful for the Bergs' hospitality.

Mrs. Berg worked part-time for Gary for a number of years, and she still does his bookkeeping. She met Gary at a community art show in 1975 and bought some pieces of his sculpture. A teacher who left the field in order to raise a family, Mrs. Berg responded to Gary's request that she work for him.

"He's very quiet, and in the early years, it was difficult to get information from him," said Mrs. Berg, who feels her forte is not in creative writing, but in concise, factual writing that effectively introduced Gary and his work to the media and potential exhibitors and collectors.

"I thought of my role as that initial push, telling people this sculpture was new, exciting, different and worthwhile. I didn't care to write articles myself; I sent out a press kit to encourage writers to do their own stories; I wanted to ensure that each article turned out to be unique. From the Middlesex County College and other college shows, I enjoyed watching Jim's career grow into the national museum network."

Mrs. Berg's husband James also contributed to the promotion of Gary's art by bringing wallhangings and other pieces to the attention of the executives at Riverview Medical Center, Red Bank, where Berg was then an administrator. Corporate purchases resulted.

"A lot of people like Gary's sculpture—a lot of people like it but can't afford it," said Mrs. Berg. "I would say to them, 'This piece would be a focal point, something special. It's worth every dime you'd put into it and more.' Then I'd watch them crawl under Jim's tables, for example, to see how they're put together. They were fascinated."

Now a large measure of fascination is lavished on Gary's dinosaurs.

Gary's "prehistoric" sculptures, known collectively as "Twentieth-Century Dinosaurs," comprise one of the finest traveling exhibits in existence, according to Douglas R. Noble, director of the Memphis Pink Palace Museum, Tennessee, in 1982.

His 1982 show at the Memphis Pink Palace Museum drew the largest number of visitors in the museum's 53 years of existence; more than 70,000 in ten weeks, Noble documented.

Hundreds of thousands of viewers attended his show in the People's Museum, Tokyo, Japan, in the spring of 1984. The Los Angeles County Museum of Natural History boasted more than 500,000 spectators in twelve weeks due to the infinite magnetism of his Twentieth-Century Dinosaurs.

"It certainly proved to be one, if not *the,* most popular special exhibit we have ever had," wrote Leon G. Arnold, assistant director of the Los Angeles County Museum.

"The Jim Gary exhibit was very successful with about a 300-percent increase over the same time one year previous," wrote John B. Clark, director of the Bruce Museum, Greenwich, Connecticut, in 1979. The media "loved the show because it is very photogenic. It has tremendous grass roots appeal."

The list of museums that have successfully mounted Jim Gary's compelling metal-sculpture show is increasing, and Gary insists upon maintaining his own system to deal with the artworld.

His "system" is to defy all established trails to one-man exhibitions in major museums. Instead of the typical representation by a gallery, Gary sends to museum directors a motley packet of photographs of his work, published clippings and tearsheets, previous exhibit data, and a résumé too overloaded with credits for even the most liberal of résumé standards. His portfolio—a 20″ x 30″ relic with a broken zipper—runneth over.

Museums throughout the United States as well as other corners of the world want the show. Gary's sculptures attract "small children to their grandparents, from artists to our own research paleontologists," said Timothy Parks, assistant director of the Carnegie Museum of Natural History, Carnegie Institute, Pittsburgh, where Gary brought his artwork in 1982.

"Floridians are still talking about Jim Gary," wrote Walter L. Smith, president of Florida A&M University, Tallahassee, in August 1978. "Without a doubt, (Gary's) exhibition…was one of the most creative and popular artistic acts ever to hit the city of Tallahassee. We estimate that 212,000 people saw the work during my Inauguration Weekend…. Appearances by (Gary) on evening and night TV news shown on WECA and CBS-affiliate WCTV-TV reached an additional 173,000 people…. It was truly an entertaining, informative and educational experience for all of us."

Incongruous as well with the artworld is the sculpture itself—huge, anatomically correct dinosaurs of all species that push the philosophy of *objet trouvé* to the limit. Gary's major medium consists of oil pans, brake shoes, rocker arms, push rods, universal joints, leaf springs, and other discarded car parts from the auto graveyards of Monmouth County, New Jersey.

Save Gary's playful use of automobile paint (a shocking-pink Pteranodon, a yellow or an earth-toned Stegosaurus, for examples), the sculptures swing from art to science to technology like a high-powered pendulum. Museums of natural history and museums of art mount Jim Gary's show, a lot which falls to few artists. Gary's show, for instance, opened the Charleston Museum of Art in South Carolina. Also, "it is enormously difficult for history/natural history museums to obtain high-quality, three-dimensional, traveling exhibits. Although Twentieth-Century Dinosaurs is not a natural history exhibit in the strictest sense, it is one of the finest traveling displays I have seen in my ten years as a museum director," wrote Douglas Noble in 1982. "Any museum with an adequate marketing plan and promotion will captivate the imagination of the entire community and can fully expect the same success we experienced."

Twentieth-Century Dinosaurs bring life and motion to what may be a stagnant "museum" atmosphere with their "personalities." Their facial expressions range from ferocious to bewildered, from daffy to determined. In these traits, they are undeniably the offspring of Jim Gary—it's practically genetic.

One can find Gary's art on the pages of science periodicals *(National Geographic World, Ranger Rick, The Explorer),* trade journals *(Welding, Ford Times, U.S. Steel, Auto Week, Games),* and art magazines such as *N.J. Music & Arts,* which put Gary's sculpture, "Red Bird," on the cover. In a *New York Times* article, Chester H. Newkirk, director of the Morris Museum, Morristown, N.J., 1979, called Gary's work "spectacular." Features about his work were flagged across the Milwaukee daily newspaper when his record-breaking show was at the Milwaukee Public Museum in May 1984.

Museum house organs, such as *Terra* of the Los Angeles County Museum, spotlight Gary's celebrated collection of dinosaurs. Museums whose budgets are expanded by corporate sponsors especially enjoy all the bonfires in the media that Gary's show ignites.

Not only does Gary provide a flaming exhibit, but the lectures, demonstrations, slide shows, personal appearances on radio and TV, newspaper interviews, and museum-generated related programs add what John Clark noted as "impact and excitement" to the show.

"People have been calling and coming in with great disappointment to find that (Gary's) sculptures were no longer with us," Clark wrote.

Mildred S. Compton, executive director of The Children's Museum, Indianapolis, wrote in a 1980 letter to Gary:

"As you know, we invited you to have your exhibit here for the winter months as we had declining visitation in this period during the last two years. This year we are pleased that we have had over 116,500 visitors during the period of your exhibition. This has set a record for that period!

"(Twentieth-Century Dinosaurs) is the first exhibit which we have had for which we received universally excellent comments from all segments of our visitors."

It took Twentieth-Century Dinosaurs precisely two days after opening on July 1, 1985, at the California Academy of Sciences of San Francisco, to break all museum attendance statistics of the past 140 years.

While the world expects artists to be as flamboyant as Salvador Dali, Gary can be reserved and self-effacing. He usually wears jeans and T-shirts on which "Twentieth-Century Dinosaurs" logos have been silkscreened. Under duress, Gary will wear a tie, but only ties with little dinosaurs on them. When photographed with his sculpture or called upon to take a public bow, Gary said he feels "like a turkey."

Moreover, Gary does not want to be known only as a *black* artist, and sometimes he will turn down ethnic-group programs.

"I don't do ethnic art," Gary said. "My work has no bearing on my being black. My sculpture is good in all colors. Remember that birds are brightly colored."

Gary's sculptures—prehistoric and contemporary—are as colorful and surprising a spectacle as Nature herself, and viewers can't get enough of them.

Many of the articles and TV shows about Gary such as "Real People" and "Prime Time" emphasize that he "recycles" old car parts in this era of diminishing resources. Just as Picasso created "Head of a Bull" with a bicycle seat and handlebars, so does Gary make an immediate history of discards. While the pieces Gary uses in his sculptures are recognizable, he wants the viewer to see first the sculpture, first the art.

"At my Charleston Museum show, a woman asked me if she could purchase a 'dinosaur kit' for her grandson to assemble," Gary said. The woman had no idea that Gary's complicated creations began not with Krazy Glue and a set of directions, but with predatorial prowls for pieces "that fit my design," as Gary put it.

David Timidaiski, Jr., Colts Neck, owned a shop where Gary went to have parts of his bicycles and other "vehicles" welded until he taught Gary to weld them himself. Timidaiski recounted Gary's uncanny ability even as a teenager to assess a heap of trash and find in it parts to build go-carts (with gasoline engines) and automobiles.

"He insisted on my trying out one of his go-carts before he installed the brakes," Timidaiski said to illustrate his view of Gary as an irrepressible enthusiast, an inventor who is part artist, part engineer.

"As I zoomed down the road, the steering wheel came off in my hand. The cart took me across my mother's lawn to run down one of her trees. The cart stopped and hung at the bank of the reservoir." One of Timidaiski's friends who witnessed his joyride minus a steering-wheel pin, was besieged by laughter. The penchant to test himself and his creation has led Gary down a difficult, but often merry, road. From outdoor art shows to museum exhibitions, Gary's work is still lacking (by Gary's own hand) metaphorical brakes.

His intricate sculptures stop at nothing within the boundaries, if there are any, of imagination.

Despite the magnitude of appreciation Gary's work gathers, there is always an enchanted viewer who simply cannot place the work in its proper category.

"Some people will always ask me, 'What do you call this?' 'Sculpture,' I say. Then they ask, 'Do you also do art?' It's amazing to hear things like this. I try not to look surprised," Gary said.

Instead, Gary looks at his busy schedule. For all his breaking of rules and hybrid work, he thrives on touring with his "entourage"— beautiful, daft, and totally art. His life now is a far cry from his early days in Colts Neck.

Gary struggled and wrenched away from a background that seemed to hold no special future for him, from his parents to the Sterners' dismay with his pursuit of sculpture as a career.

Gary's natural parents had died, and E. Donald Sterner, whom he called his "Dad," died at the age of 89 on September 30, 1983.

Sterner held many public positions, including that of a state assemblyman (1928), a state senator (1930) and chairman of the Republican State Committee (1933). He was best known for serving as New Jersey's first highway commissioner, appointed by Gov. Harold G. Hoffman in 1935.

While in these posts, Sterner was instrumental in providing funds for many bridges in the Central New Jersey area, and for the development of the Belmar marina, whose administration building was named in honor of Sterner's outstanding public service.

Sterner's obituary appeared on Page One of the Asbury Park Press. His devotion to civic affairs and the Boy Scouts was mentioned; his connection with Jim Gary was not. Gary was left feeling that Sterner never quite understood him or his art. He recalled Sterner asking him for years, "Did you get a job yet, or are you still bending wire?"

"Jimmy was a nice child," said Dorothy Sterner, now 74 and residing in Avon-By-The-Sea after 40 years in Colts Neck. Her tone was guarded, the voice of one not yet convinced her former charge's creations are held in artistic esteem far and wide.

"He was never lazy. He earned every cent he ever made," she said. "Jimmy was always mechanical—good with his hands, the most ambitious of all his family. He took care of the house and the dogs when we were away, and he was always around me when I was cooking in the kitchen. As a young child, he went to dumps to buy car parts and old motors, and he worked on them till they were running. We were very fond of him."

Trips to salvage yards have been an enduring portion of Gary's life as a teenager who built three cars from the ground up before he had a license to drive and as a sculptor who finds it increasingly difficult to acquire what are now antiquated automobile parts. New cars boast either plastic mechanisms or redesigned metal parts that have none of

the form and character of the parts of old Cadillacs, Lincolns, and Chevrolets, alas, the contemporary "dinosaurs."

That in his safaris for scrap metal and mechanical parts Gary began to see segments of animal physiology bespeaks his gift for spatial relationships and design, major tools of the sculptor. He makes no studies save the *in toto* design in his head, and he works painstakingly and cumulatively as though he were the subject of the children's rhyme, "The House That Jack Built," until the mental design actually stands before him. If the air compressor won't work, Gary sets out to repair it, and if the tool to repair it with is broken, he sets out to fix the tool, and so on in a chain of a work process that would try the patience of the Shoemaker's elves.

It is not extraordinary, then, to know that the "great tinkerer" Rube Goldberg awarded Gary the "Best-in-Show" prize in the Atlantic City Boardwalk Show in 1966 for his collage "Signs of the Times," finding in Gary a part of himself.

Florence V. Miller, chairman of the Atlantic City Fine Arts Commission, executive director of the Atlantic City Arts Center and holder of many titles in the city's cultural atmosphere, said Gary is one of her all-time favorites. "I like to think we had a part in starting off his success," Mrs. Miller said. "I always held my breath until he got here at the shows." Gary's drivenness results in a repertoire of sculpture that appears effortless, like a ballet, to the unsuspecting eye.

Viewers stroll from one gallery to another within the walls of a revered institution—the Museum.

They hope to expand their lungs with airborne culture and permeate their brains with intellectual cells. The very environs of the museum cause guests to whisper and ponder and move with poise or sit on a bench mesmerized by the profundity either hanging or standing.

Did anyone ever think of what the exhibition hall looked like during the installation of the show? Or how the show got there in the first place?

Gary's museum exhibitions came from his studio in Hightstown, New Jersey—an off-the-beaten-track, almost hermetic location for Twentieth-Century Dinosaurs. Know above all that these metal sculptures are huge, some almost 50 feet long and as high as a house. They are loaded onto a 48-foot flatbed trailer in pieces, which Gary must reassemble at the museum. Each part is hoisted with a Rube Goldberg-type crane, Gary's original fusion of half-car, half-forklift. Sometimes an angry Allosaurus can be seen swinging in the breeze six feet from the ground as Gary drives his crane through the dirt. A Stegosaurus of substantial might has been known to crash into the crane when "in flight" and take a nasty bite out of the crane.

"I build things big," Gary said, "so I have to have special tables, bending tools and stands to hold the pieces while I'm working on them. And I need a crane to move them. I couldn't afford to buy all that equipment, so I had to make it with pulleys, hydraulic mechanisms from trucks, motors, gears, and other metal—also from the junkyard. Parts for the crane cost me about $100, as opposed to the several thousand dollars I would have spent if I had to buy one. I used part of a 1968 Pontiac, truck metal to make the boom (the lifting arm), chains and hooks.

"Before I made the crane, I counted on friends to help me move the sculpture, but I worried that something would fall on them. I relied on lifting using ramps, levers, bars and muscle like the Ancient Romans."

Gary's crane is guest of honor, however, during photographic sessions. A photographer requests that a sculpture be placed in a field among dried plant stalks and gray debris. Then, she requests that Gary use a fogger to produce a thick smoky mist around the dinosaur. "More!" she demands. "Keep it smoking!" The fog approaches London proportions but the dinosaur maintains its photogenicity, hot lights or smog or plastic bag over its head.

While Gary's dinosaurs are unerring models, they must be transported with great attention to every detail. They were scheduled for a six-month exhibit in Tokyo, Japan, for example, and an export company based in the World Trade Center, New York, was engaged. The dinosaurs would be packed into Sea-Land trailers, disassembled, tagged, color-coded and photo-coded for reassembly at destination, anchored and padded to minimize damage, and shipped across the Pacific. At sea for approximately a month, the Twentieth-Century Dinosaurs exhibit insured against all conceivable risks including government seizure and war.

On land, Gary's regular driver, Bryan Culbertson of Lebanon, Ohio, hauls the tons of artwork with an ingenuous relish of the atypical load. The tractor-trailer again must be loaded. In order to conserve space and get as many sculptures as possible to his Anniston (Alabama) Museum show, Gary built large shelves into the trailer itself. The sculptor must also be an engineer to accommodate all pieces, from the two-foot wing span of a Dragonfly to a 20-foot-high Platosaurus.

Once the sculptures arrive at the site of exhibition, Gary insists upon repainting them and sprucing them up for their admirers, much like shining and oiling the Tin Man before he is fit to see the Wizard of Oz. And Gary is wont to lug air-compressors, welding torch, many cans of paint, spray guns, and tools wherever goeth his dinosaurs. Traveling light is unheard of.

After the dinosaurs are impeccably groomed, the next task is to situate each of them in the museum and on museum grounds. The entire museum staff gets involved, by now exasperated by the feverish pace Jim Gary has set. Forklift in motion, the sculptures are strategically placed for optimum drama. This can take days before the official opening and reception of the show. Champagne and compliments, after all, must be earned. All manipulations are strictly backstage once the public starts pouring in.

Not even members of the media have an inkling of the ruckus that went on until the eleventh hour before presentation.

Gary not only worries about how his sculptures look in the museum, but about the entire atmosphere of a show, from formal to "down home." One museum served beer in cans (up for grabs in a bucket), hamburgers, and potato chips at the opening reception.

"All we needed were ants and we could have had a picnic," Gary said.

The media who descend upon the fascinating sculptures and the elusive Jim Gary also need to be addressed.

Many writers, in their excitement over the non-traditional sculpture, want to create new descriptions of Gary's art. They call the sculptures "junkyard art," "metal monsters," "car-part creatures," "scrappy creatures"—anything but just *sculpture*. Reporters sent to cover Gary's show are not always art historians, but they make sincere and enthusiastic efforts to bring the impact of Gary's art to the greatest number of readers. Reporters may also ask questions that have nothing to do with art or sculpture—"How old are you, Mr. Gary?" "Are you married, Mr. Gary?" "With whom did you study, Mr. Gary?"

Mr. Gary refuses to answer. He is, the public should know, old enough, married to his work, and self-taught. Of his personal life there is no more information unless Gary decides it is appropriate. A biographer would have to be an astute detective as opposed to relying on Gary's offerings.

The public should also know that Gary likes it this way. He wants only to be known for his sculpture, not for "the shy, easy smile" that reporters invariably report. During the installation of the exhibit, the shy, easy smile is harder to come by. It is aggravating to have to stay abreast of each museum's particular climate and every aspect of the show. Gary's brow does furrow, though he was known for a few pranks in his youth. (David Timidaiski said one Halloween, Gary borrowed a ladder from a local orchard and used it to put the Timidaiskis' lawn furniture on their roof.) A sense of humor is ever-present, and Gary can charm museum personnel and corporate officials, friends and strangers.

Corporations helping to fund a show, for instance, is another aspect with which Gary must contend. Sometimes a corporation helping the museum to pay expenses wishes to have its own separate exhibit in conjunction with that in the museum. Gary is then required to place sculptures there and negotiate insurance matters, adjunct publicity, and purchasing. Because no two corporations are alike,

there is no mastering the job.

From dealing with corporations and companies outside the museum, Gary has learned that a new and challenging quirk will crop up every time. The artist who benefits from company funds must maintain his dignity and standards while appreciating the support. At times, executing these two efforts is like being on the North and South Poles at once. Without the corporations, however, the sculptures may not be exhibited. As always, the dinosaurs keep their cool and withstand whatever environment with aplomb.

They can also loftily avoid scheduling problems. Gary's traveling exhibit is often booked one to two years in advance via contract between him and the museum. Lecture-demonstrations, art and science events, exhibits and media presentations from TV shows to publications tend to fall into the short-notice category. Then see how the dinosaurs run. Madcap sculpting, sprucing, and publicity-package sprees involve energy that would confound Con Edison.

Gary is a compulsive artist. Knowing that sculptures must arrive in Philadelphia for the opening of a museum's new Discovering Dinosaurs hall and for an exhibit at Field Museum, Chicago, and for another show at Boston Museum all in the same time span, Gary will work non-stop for days. He himself is a strange dinosaur, able to construct a mammoth using the gifted right hemisphere of his brain (the seat of spacial-relationship abilities) as well as physical brawn. The metal parts—Gary has used as many as 500 in one sculpture—are heavy. Welding is hard work. Getting a sculpture to stand free without fear of keeling over means that Gary use special buttressing until the engineering techniques take hold.

Long before the welder's torch is in his hand, Gary must cruise the auto graveyards, excavate for suitable pieces or purchase brand new pieces, and load them into a battleship of a Dodge van. Then unloading, welding, shaping, sandblasting, and painting.

The only breaks Gary allows himself when the schedule is asphyxiating are brief snoozes in a chair and taking in a movie. The work gets done miraculously, because Gary will not, considering the magnitude of the plans, let a museum (or anyone) down. Every detail is anticipated and executed with clockwork precision. His shows draw stupendous crowds--certainly no one could say that Twentieth-Century Dinosaurs are unreliable.

Even though they were not responsible for standing at just the right angle, for shocking viewers with their unusual color (it's not easy being a pink Eryops), for being marvelously touchable, the dinosaur sculptures get all the credit.

Lighting? Surrounding plants, gardens, and fountains? Billboards? Posters? Banners? Someone to sweep and dust? Caterers for the reception? Ticket-takers and head counts? Security guards?

Why, there's practically nothing to consider when a museum presents a changing exhibit. It's as easy as falling off a dinosaur!

Once the sculptures are on display, the entire museum comes alive.

Susan Gunther, an art student who knew Gary through her family, wrote about his work to fulfill a requirement for a term paper. The course was Art 100. Entitled "Jim Gary: 'A Sculptor of Junk,' " the paper was written in 1974, nearing the end of the fall semester. The tone of the paper is not scholarly, though Ms. Gunther did include footnotes and a bibliography. It is rather a homespun and genuine tribute to Gary, perhaps not unlike what some of Gary's admirers at the museums may be thinking.

Despite some biographical inaccuracies, Ms. Gunther's work is as follows:

Jim Gary, a contemporary metal sculptor, made a bird that is "alive," out of junk that was "dead." I saw it, and I was impressed. I chose to write my paper on a contemporary artist, one with whom I could speak personally, because my knowledge in the field of art is limited, yet I am appreciative of talent in any form. Jim's talent is uniquely expressed, and because of that quality, I found studying his work even more stimulating. It is far greater to enter a man's workshop, see his work, touch his work, than to open a book and merely gaze upon it.

There is not a vast amount of information written about "junk art." Since Jim has only recently, within the past two years, seriously looked into the works of men such as David Smith, a pioneer in scrap-metal sculpture, it made it even more difficult to relate his talent with others in his field. Jim's main reason for shying away from artists related to his work was to insure originality of his own ideas. Jim, therefore, was not influenced by another artist, but rather, through his own experiences he was able to arrive at his present form of expression.

Jim was born, raised and now resides in New Jersey. When was he born? Well, if the information is that important, I guess you'll have to ask him yourself. Jim simply grinned, and conveniently withheld the information. Fortunately, I believe he is young enough to have plenty of time to "create." *In fact, if the saying, "You're not getting older, you're getting better" applies to Mr. Gary, the world of sculpture is in for some real treats!*

Jim feels that it is time to get sculpture up and out of the cellar and brought up to the show standards of painting. In some areas, a first place painter will receive twice as much as a first place sculptor. At one time, sculpture was, "a glorious public art, capable of sustaining the scrutiny of the crowd, robust enough to stand its ground amid the tumult of modern life."[1] Work, such as Jim's, is attempting to bring the standards of sculpture back up to where they belong. (Ms. Gunther refers to several art shows which offered less prize money for sculpture than for paintings, which Gary protested by packing up and leaving.) However, his ultimate goal is to gain national, as well as local and state, recognition as an artist and a sculptor.

As a boy in his teens, Jim was intrigued with cars, and he actually built two from the "ground up." While sorting through numerous piles of machine parts for the car he was making, he became aware of their value as form. In the manual arts course at Freehold Regional High School, Jim gained experience that further developed his sense of form and volume. It was there that he discovered his artistic talents.

After high school, Jim spent some years in the Navy. I am quite sure it was some time before Jim realized the value of his naval experiences. I say this with some confidence since I cannot help but recall a comment Jim made one day at my folk's house concerning his Navy life. "Sure, Join the Navy, see the world—through a porthole!!" Although at that time his view of the "world" had been narrowed, the view of his future, which was yet to be realized, was only beginning to broaden.

After the Navy, Jim was a processor in the Job Corps where he also helped young people in a welding course. In an attempt to keep the students occupied with something different to do, he began creating. Up until this point, Jim had fooled around making Christmas decorations from scrap metal, such as a wreath from old beer cans. But it was his effort at finding something for the kids to do in the welding class in the Job Corps that truly inspired him.

Presently, Jim is the owner and operator of the Iron Butterfly Art Studio and Gallery which originated in Colts Neck in 1968. He relocated the Iron Butterfly to Red Bank in February of 1970. His objective is to stimulate the aesthetic feeling of everyone through his work. This is accomplished through lectures, demonstrations, television and news media, and exhibits.

For Jim, a junkyard is his art supply store. In fact, ninety-nine percent of his materials were rescued from a junk pile. The H & H Junkyard in Marlboro Township is preferred since Jim can wander around himself in search of the necessary "parts." There was a time when junk was free, but those days are gone. (Bobby Howard, owner of H & H, went out of his way to save parts or let Gary know something special came in. Howard, quick with a joke, had an unspoken appreciation for Gary's art.)

The base is the sculptor's convention for rooting his art to surrounding reality while permitting it to stand apart.[2] It says, in effect, that the sculpture has a life, a "presence" of its own.[3] Its use to support various top-heavy standing figures, and to provide a perch to minimize damage, are the obvious physical reasons for its existence; beyond that, the base helps to create an aura of distance and dignity around the object.[4] Two trends have dominated the modern base: the first incorporates the base into the sculpture itself, to the point where the sculpture rests directly on the floor or ground; the second attempts to free sculpture from all earthly contact or means of visible support, making sculpture not so much airborne as gravity defying.[5] David Smith, a principle master of this genre, was inclined, for the most part, toward forms of a figurelike verticality.[6] Even his landscapes were mounted on pedestal "feet."[7]

Much of Jim Gary's work takes the form of large birds and animals done in a free-standing style with the sculpture resting directly on the ground. From my observations, Jim's use of the base is limited to support. In fact, even the wall murals Jim creates appear suspended in air! Anthony Caro's sensibility generally expressed itself in a landscape-like horizontality.[8] However, into this he projected a similar form of Cubist drawing—what used to be called drawing-in-space—which effectively eliminates the pedestal (real or imagined) in order to root his forms in the ground itself.[9] Mark diSuvero, a sculptor who used rough wooden beams, iron chains, and painted steel sections, also did not feel confined to a tidy base or discreet pedestal which forced the sculpture to rise, figurelike, on a mass that left the surrounding space expressively uninvolved.[10]

Jean Tinguely has come closest to "humanizing" the machine.[11] He felt that to be "human" was to expose oneself through animal vulnerability and fallibility.[12] To prove this, he created machines designed to perform absurd tasks, yet

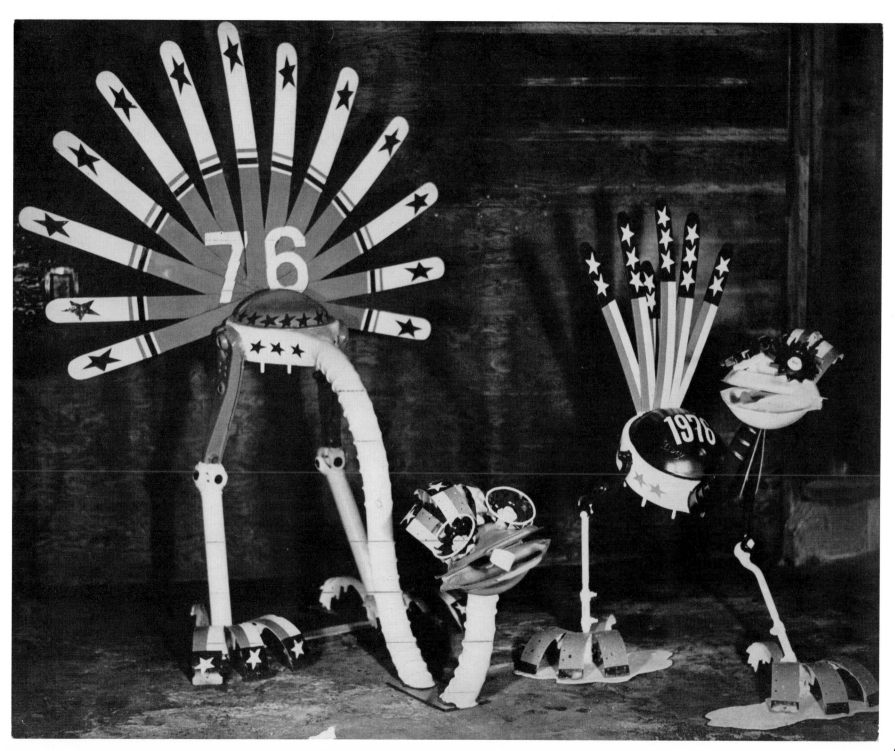

fully aware that the chances of the machine succeeding were few.[13] Tinguely's sculptures are actually demented contraptions that shimmy, grind and pound themselves toward extinction and a return to the junk from which they were born.[14]

The future is considerably brighter for Jim Gary's sculptures. In one respect, however, they are similar, for Jim has "humanized" the parts of a machine. His ulterior motive is not to show the "breaking down" of a machine, but rather the creation of yet another form. Each piece of "junk" is reconstructed even though you can still tell what it was, and the pieces are put together with a lasting purpose or design in mind. This technique of Jim's can be paralleled with David Smith's idea that every work becomes, at least in part, a clear exposition of the way it has been made.[15] Smith felt that structure and image were reciprocal and indissoluble, and that the sculptor's fantasy was completely assimilated to the technology of his method.[16]

Jim uses practically every part of an automobile except the engine block. Beer cans, washers, springs, nuts and bolts —just about everything people have around their homes collecting dust are all found in intricate designs as a part of Jim's sculpture. His favorite creations are the animals, especially the birds. Why? Jim likes animals. The average bird's anatomy consists of the following parts—all from an automobile: oil pan covers for the head, break shoes for the tail and, quite appropriately, the feet, steering linkage for the legs, and rear-end housing for the neck and body. A "peacock" is a bit more delicate. A metal grass rake is used for the tail, copperwire for the plumage, fan blades for the wings, water pump housing for the neck, and steel rods for the legs. The most amazing part of all was that first I saw a peacock, and then I saw a rake. That is exactly what was supposed to happen, which is why his work is great—and believable.

Somehow, Jim's talent has enabled him to take hard metal and make it appear soft. Although evident in his animal forms, it is an outstanding quality of his "Universal Woman," a life-size torso assembled from hundreds of metal washers, welded one by one, edge to edge. The lines of her body are unmistakably soft—except to the touch.

In Jim's work, realism vs. the abstract. He deals with real things such as a bird, a woman's body, Christmas, a cross, but in an abstract, not quite tangible sense. His sculpture has kept in touch with our everyday lives, yet he is capable of taking it one step further. This is one of the reasons Jim feels his work to be unique in its field. There were, and are,

other junk artists. However, Jim's "creations" are truly his, and original besides.

Just as Jim has his favorite sculptures, the animals, he also has pieces of sculpture that he is not enthusiastic about making. One such piece is a wall mural consisting of many "starbursts" made from polished nails. It was one of the first things he ever did, and only required a few hours to construct. Jim uses this, table tops, and a few other pieces to fall back on when he needs them, since they are good sellers. However, when cash is needed to do the things Jim wants to do, there are times when he must first do the sculptures he would rather not!

Jim has a design in mind all the time he is working and does not depend on accidents to achieve a finished work. "I see lots of beauty in dark steel. There are all kinds of subtle shades and tones." To Jim, rusted steel is great. Generally Jim approaches a junkyard with a definite idea in mind and in search of the materials for making the idea a reality.

David Smith and Anthony Caro wanted to take sculpture off its precious pedestal, arrange it "non-hierarchically" on the ground, and force the viewer to see it on its own terms.[17] After seeing much of Jim's work and talking with him, I feel that Jim, also, wishes his sculpture to be viewed squarely for what it symbolically is.

When I saw a picture of a creation by Claes Oldenburg entitled "Soft Engine,"[18] which is self-explanatory, I immediately contrasted it to Jim's "Iron Butterfly." A butterfly should be soft, and an engine should be hard. Yet, when I considered it a while longer, I paralleled the two. Both men made something that was once hard, for Jim the metal, into something soft. The "Iron Butterfly" for Jim, however, has become a kind of trademark which he works into each piece he produces as a signature.

Although Jim's studio is in Red Bank, New Jersey, his workshop is in Farmingdale at the site of an abandoned chicken coop. Jim works as the spirit moves him, sometimes for days at a time with few breaks. His schedule is anything but!! For much of Jim's work, the welding, protective clothing and goggles are required. Even with the proper shoes, sparks get in and burn the socks. If the shield is lifted too soon, the sparks fly and can burn holes in his glasses and teeth. Besides being hot work, it sounds rather dangerous!!!

Jim's gimmick is to attempt to figure out something different that no one else had, something of his own—something that he likes and that someone else will like. His idea is to get art where a family can afford it. Jim wants his things out

where the average family can afford it. "A Gary sculpture in every home" is what keeps his prices down. Jim, as do all artists, wants a following, and in order to get one, his sculptures must be "accessible" to the masses.

Although Jim received no formal art training, his suggestion to young artists is to seek some kind of art school but only for the techniques. Students should avoid becoming a copy of the instructor and be prepared to sacrifice a lot for their art.

I learned a great deal from writing this paper. But mostly I am amazed at how Jim can possibly conjure up these images and then actually construct them from junk. Excuse me. "Junk"—?—is there such a thing? I now hesitate to refer to anything in such a raw term. Jim's talent for recyling junk, (there's that term again), not only places him in a category with artists, but also among the ecologists of our time.

I touched an iron butterfly, I saw the universal woman, and I anticipate—more. Thank you, Jim.

At the time Ms. Gunther wrote her term paper, Twentieth-Century Dinosaurs had not yet been created, though they were to become a most unusual staple of Gary's repertoire. Joseph Bienstock, who remembers Gary's years in Howell, said it was interesting to see how the animal sculptures evolved. "He found himself—and he found a niche for himself as a sculptor," Bienstock said. That oil pans and brake shoes and other automobile parts registered in his mind as parts of animals is a clue to Gary's childhood interest—like that of millions of children—in prehistoric life.

In *Running Free*, a Scott, Foresman and Company reading textbook published this year, a chapter entitled "Jim Gary's Giants" by Sallie A. Luther addresses some of Gary's other reasons for his creations.

"I have always wanted to be different—you know, somebody special," says Gary. "At first I sold the things I made in sidewalk sales and little art shows. Then I started entering art contests. I wanted to win. I had to be the best.

"Before long I was working harder and harder. But now it wasn't just to win. It had gotten to be for the beauty of what I was doing."

Gary goes on to say that he would look at the piles of auto parts and be reminded of animal skeletons. He wanted to make those skeletons "come alive" again.

Then Gary realized that he wanted his work to mean even more. He wanted it to stand for something. He wanted to show that many people waste too much, throw away too many things. By making his giants from junk, Gary was demonstrating that many things can be recycled.

The chapter ends with questions and suggestions for projects to check the students' comprehension and reading skills. Interestingly, the editors of the volume chose Jim Gary, along with a clarinetist with the Chicago Symphony and a writer of a radio play, as primary examples of people who express themselves as artists, and who may become role models for the young people reading about them. Sculptor Jim Gary, then, has become part of the American reading tradition, an artist "to grow up on" and be familiar with from the time one is in grade school. This is an unusual achievement considering that the lives and work of the world's artists tend to be the specialty of college art history and art appreciation courses.

Gary's work is not confined to the American youngster, however. Children in Japan ran up to him on the street and asked for autographs. They had seen him on television and in magazines before Gary began his six-month tour of museums in Tokyo and other cities.

One kindergarten class in Saudi Arabia read about Twentieth-Century Dinosaurs in *Ranger Rick* magazine, which is distributed internationally, and decided to write Gary a letter:

```
Rahima Academy
ACC Ju'aymah
Dhahran,Saudi Arabia
November 17,1983

Dear Mr. Gary,
    We liked your dinosaursvery much. And we would like you to come
visit us some day and make a dinosaur for us,a play one.
    We have lots of crashed cars here you can use!
    You could come with us to the beach and see if you can find
some things to use there.

Sincerely,
```

Kindergarten class

Josh
Alan Annabelle
Biko
Jehad Marie
Mariza Dias Tadoy
Mrs. Jacoby

This year, children in Australia will go in droves to see the exhibit at the Australian Museum, Sydney, the Queensland Museum, Brisbane, and the South Australia Museum, Adelaide. With all the young people go parents, teachers—adults as professionals and laymen, who will be as impressed as their charges. But too many comments people make are limited to "knowing what I like" and "liking what I know." Gary's art calls for imaginative explanations, perhaps along the lines of the review by Louis de Furia, publisher, in *N.J. Music & Arts,* January 1978. Of Gary's creations

questions seem to form of their own volition. Is the Dodo bird extinct or just in hiding? Here? Would Edsel parts fit? Is the minimalist saying more and more with less and less, or less and less with least? What brought Calder from mobile to stabile?...

Consciously or not, his forms have become fanciful adaptations, without the scientific appelations of Dinosaur, Brontosaurus and Dimetrodon, and stand as Orange Bird, Bird, Bug, etc. Children's toys? Hardly. Automotive novelties? Don't be silly.

To be concerned with and entrapped by which "parts" he used to construct a body or tail is to admire the stone, not the sculptor's concepts; the painting pigments and formula, not the insight of the painter.

Which brings us to the core. The spoofs are pap to entertain us and to point out that Gary is more than the sum of parts, even if they are auto parts! I questioned him about statements or reactions his work might have elicited from professional art teachers. None has gone beyond, "The children enjoyed your show." Good for the kids, but wouldn't you think a pro would lift his/her eyes beyond the brake shoes? Maybe less IS more. Shall we try a bronzed brake shoe on a neo-classical pedestal ten feet high and call it *Movement in Arrest, Opus One?* Would it then be? Be what? What we want or are conditioned to expect?

De Furia's passion for feeling the art, as opposed to scraping its most obvious layer or dusting its tip with the lightest of touches, is now in forum. For Gary's work, especially the dinosaur collection, it is about time as well as timely. One day, when rocker arms from old Chevrolets are barely recognizable in the wake of speeding technology, people will view the sculptures as sheer striking design, cutting into space in engaging ways. The pieces will be worth scrutiny and pondering titled or untitled. This is the ultimate goal of most sculptors whether they've dug deeply enough to express it aloud or not. Gary expressed it years ago.

While many of Gary's sculpted forms are indelibly identifiable—specifically or generically—they take on ironic new attitudes, again, to be felt more than seen. Exemplary is "The Chicken" by Jim Gary and writer David Shirey's critique of it in *The New York Times,* August 8, 1976:

"A folksier, more homespun object, a hearthside keepsake is Jim Gary's welded-steel rooster, a bionic fowl put together, I believe, with what-nots that the artist happened to find in treasure hunts. This cock is all cockalorum, a country bumpkin with more braggadocio than any hayseed, cornball Napolean imaginable."

Other art critics and writers "feel" Gary's work by carrying its varied titles (or captions, as the case may be) beyond reality and into a playful joust with fantasy. Susan Orlean wrote in *The Boston Phoenix,* February 5, 1985, of her fact-is-stranger-than-fiction reactions to Gary's sculpture.

I hit an awful traffic jam on the way over and had to stop for gas besides. My brakes were making a funny noise, and the raw spot on my passenger door—caused by the unexpected visit of someone bent on heisting my briefcase—was rusting by the minute. Then I couldn't find a parking space. I know, I know—if I lived here, I'd be home by now. But this was business, and I was determined, at any cost, to see New Jersey sculptor Jim Gary give a demonstration at the (Boston) Museum of Science.

Gary builds almost-lifesize metal dinosaurs, and he makes them out of old car parts. Leaky oil pan giving you a headache? Imagine it as a brontosaurus head. Had enough of your rod-end caps? Vertebrae. Rocker arms giving out? There are iguanodon feet in your future. Sick of the whole damned bucket of bolts? Dump your bad Detroit dream in Red Bank, New Jersey, and Jim Gary may make you a star....

The completed Gary dinosaurs are big skeletal creatures with little bony hands and quizzical expressions on their oil-pan heads. They are more or less anatomically correct; the car parts, once translated into dinosaur, don't look much like pieces of that

four-on-the-floor deuce-and-a-quarter ragtop with breath and slides that you always dreamed about. They look like bones.

Ms. Orlean caught Gary's entire act in her rollicking mock-cynicism. Under humorous subtitles—"Little GTOsaur," "Little deuce couposaur," and "Little red Corvettodon"—she drew from Gary's messages in his art directly and placed them on the tightrope stretching from recognition to interpretation.

Writer Nels Nelson also came forward with an aggressive account of the dinosaurs' and Gary's impact (he included statements about other sculpture by Gary as though he were obligated to bring his readers the whole picture). As Gary installed the dinosaur show at the Academy of Natural Sciences in Philadelphia, Nelson noted that "passing strangers reacted uniformly. Each and every one of them registered (1) double-take, (2) disbelief and (3) delight. What artist could ask for more?"

To the obvious merit of the work Nelson added: "Jim Gary's no amateur. No fly-by-night. Self-taught, he has been creating his so-called junkyard sculpture for some 10 years. His work graces the New Brunswick campus of Rutgers University, a public library in Phillipsburg, N.J., and several private collections. Salvage dinosaurs are only one category of his work, albeit the most incessant talkers for themselves."

He called Gary himself a "wiry and powerful man who takes his case-hardened menagerie on the road quite a lot and knows precisely what to expect. One senses that he enjoys the revelation almost as much as the creation—and very likely more, considering the work involved."

Nelson astutely picked out the polish and professionalism in Gary even though the Philadelphia exhibit in 1979 marked Gary's first museum connection. Gary had wondered if the curators would "take a chance on the show," as he put it, despite all his experience with public favor in the art shows, and his enigmatic personality already established in the local press. After a huge success, Gary was on his way to other museum personnel who would consistently honor his work and deepen his personal and artistic values.

The Philadelphia show was a landmark of Gary's values. It represented his conviction that the artwork must earn respect before it could earn a living, respect going hand-in-hand with many lean years and personal sacrifices.

He moved from what de Furia called a "chicken-coop-cum-sculpture studio" in Howell Township, N.J., to a gallery on Route 34 in Colts Neck. There he set up a place to display his works (the smaller pieces) and hold art shows and sales for local artists, including Jerry Lubeck, Herb Wiley and Toni Monks, whom he befriended, and to live, which he had to do secretly because his lease prohibited use of the space as living quarters.

After nearly four years, rents in the area near Delicious Orchards skyrocketed. Gary had been surviving on tiny commissions from other artists and art-show prize money he had won. His need to earn more money and his artistic principles were instrumental in his fight to equalize street-show prizes for painting and sculpture.

"Each artist in these shows paid the same amount of money for his space," Gary recalled. "Sculpture was treated like a craft, which I resented. I had won prizes for sculpture many times, though—it got to

be difficult for other sculptors entered in the shows. One exhibitor, Edith Hode, said, 'If Jim showed up, other sculptors felt they had no chance of winning.' I was always late, which kept them in suspense.

"I was a sore loser when it came to cliquish games of favorites," he said. "Judges started telling me they had to let someone else win this time. I protested by packing up my work and leaving the show. Eventually, the rules changed; at least sculptors could win as much prize money as any other artist."

Prizes that took the form of ribbons instead of currency meant little to Gary as well, for he told judges in these shows he couldn't live on ribbons.

Gary's struggle became apparent to several businessmen and women who appreciated his work and understood his drive to support himself on sculpture and sculpture alone. Women Gary dated, however, could not tolerate his erratic work schedule, pay arrangements and general artistic zeal during the time he had to eke by and promote his sculpture. One woman told him to get a "serious" job if he wanted her.

"People who are really good at what they do have to put blinders on to the rest of the world," Gary said in reply. "People who were going to all the parties didn't get any work done—not the same kind of work. I have a lot of friends who know they'll see me when they see me. They're the kind of people who can sustain a relationship in spite of this."

The business people formed a group called "Friends of Jim Gary" to help ease his way to making sculpture a serious job. The group from New Jersey included Edward Diamond, M.D., South Orange; Furman Templeton, Esq., East Orange; Clinton C. Crocker, director of Rutgers University Art Services, New Brunswick; Lewis Korb, Little Silver; James B. Berg, Oceanport; Minda Shein, East Brunswick; Rena Petti White, Kendall Park; William McGill, Browns Mills; Dean Sachs, director of Rutgers University Eductional Opportunities, New Brunswick; Donald Goldman, Bridgewater; Helen Moffatt, Oceanport; James Abis, Ocean Township; Sylvia Diamond, Lakewood, and Leonard Schlosberg, Tinton Falls.

They realized Gary was gathering debts while doing many a *gratis* show, and felt he must seek only paying sponsors. By this time, Gary had left the Colts Neck studio for the less expensive loft in Red Bank. The group pledged to find shows that would offer payment, but efforts never materialized and his agreement with the group—to show for ample remuneration—seemed doomed: Museums and art organizations expected to "pay" artists in prestige. Gary knew he had to take a stand if he were to amount to anything in this outlandish business.

His inspiration came to him through the music he listened to while he worked on the dinosaurs that would later become his artistic hole-in-one. Various rock groups took their shows on the road, touring from city to city, to familiarize the public with their individual sounds. Gary thought of doing exactly that to bring his work to more people. The Academy of Natural Science in Philadelphia offered him a show—*gratis*. Gary felt the exposure had the potential to send him with recommendations to other museums.

After about seven months of trying to comply with the Friends of Jim Gary tenet, he ended the association by agreeing to do the Philadelphia exhibit.

His instincts were correct; the show was a great success. In light of the attendance at the museum and major press coverage of his sculptures, Gary was able to go from the Academy to the Children's Museum in Indianapolis, which paid him for the exhibit. He made the same amount as the truck driver who hauled the show!

In the artworld, where often there is no such thing as a steady paycheck or benefits or tenure, Gary was finally on his way to managing the Twentieth-Century Dinosaurs for bread, butter, and more metal. Any marriage—save Gary's to his life as a sculptor—would not exist.

Ruth Schlosberg, of Tinton Falls, N.J., had met Gary about eighteen years ago, when the artists of Red Bank frequently opened their doors to each other and interested passers-by, forming an ad hoc writers and artist's group. Mrs. Schlosberg would wander into Gary's studio at 8 Broad Street while waiting for an hour or more for her children's dance instruction to be over. She spotted sculpture—one a large wallhanging made of welded railroad spikes—that she would eventually purchase for a small amount.

"Jim had this piece in the studio, and my husband Lenny and I had our eye on it," Mrs. Schlosberg said. "At a Christmas party in the artists' studios, Lenny asked about the piece. Jim said $50.

"We were a young couple with three little children then, and we didn't have a fast $50. So we paid in $10 installments as often as we could."

When the Schlosbergs wanted the piece in time for a party they were giving, they called Gary.

"He came with his drill two hours before the guests were to arrive. He said, 'Don't worry' and started drilling holes in the dining room wall and installed the sculpture," Mrs. Schlosberg said.

"Then he ran out to change his clothes and came back to the party. In the 1960s when we were all bohemians and flower children, that was so typical of how we did things then."

For their tenth wedding anniversary, the Schlosbergs purchased a 6-foot tall, free-form candelabra Gary made from exhaust pipes. The piece is a cherished artwork in their home, Mrs. Schlosberg said, and because of its beauty and the intricate work in it, it is undoubtedly worth many times more money than they paid for it.

Of Gary, Mrs. Schlosberg said, "He really paid his dues. He started out with nothing but unusual ideas. To have that kind of dream—to stay with it—is incredible and rare. We should all have what drives him."

As an artist herself, a member of Actors' Equity, a musical-comedy performer and an extra in films ("I got to be a policewoman and stand next to Paul Newman in 'Fort Apache, The Bronx'—but I'd be embarrassed if anyone made much of that," she said.), Mrs. Schlosberg and Gary are kindred spirits.

"I gave him lots of coffee and sympathy in the hard old days," she said. "I understand his sacrifices—he's still single—and what it's like to have people tell you you're crazy and you'll never make money. (Gary) is a very shy and sweet man. If he's your friend, he'll do anything for you. He's not a phony—he's real."

In order to cope with the real world, an artist must sustain a workable vision while he endures unpredictable turns of events. They can be stressful, good or bad, and at times both good and bad. Gary's reality is filled with these events; it is not easy to temper one's emotions as one may temper the metal that emerges as sculpture.

About eleven years ago, Gary had been invited to exhibit his work in Cherry Hill, N.J., and speak as guest artist at the opening of the show. He had just won the 1975 Artist of the Year award from the Art Educators Association of New Jersey and was a popular choice as a speaker at many art-related functions.

During the installation of the Cherry Hill Show, there was much hustle-bustle as Gary brought each piece of sculpture in and did whatever was necessary, including removing boxes and debris in the exhibit area, to create the proper environment for the viewers. As he worked, a woman approached him and said, "When you're finished putting those boxes away, come back and move this stuff for me." Gary said he would and complied with her wishes. He noticed it was getting late afterward—he had to get back to the hotel to dress for the evening's activities.

But the woman then asked him to sweep the floor. Gary said no, he had other things to do. She became indignant as he left.

At the opening ceremonies, Gary said, "I was called to the podium to accept an honor and give a speech. I happened to notice the woman I'd helped earlier—she was one of the officers of the organization hosting the show. Her face was deep red."

The woman had not met Jim Gary before and had not realized that the man who uncomplainingly lent her a hand was the guest of honor. Many people, like her, seem taken aback when they discover that the creator of unforgettable, complex artwork is black, Gary said. Even writers from magazines and newspapers, who seek stories on this sculpture that churns up whole regions with its presence, have been known to speak first to Gary's driver, Bryan Culbertson, as the two men—black and white—stood together. That Culbertson has been mistaken for the sculptor indicates to Gary the die-hard conditioning many people unwittingly employ: The white man is the artist; the black man is his assistant. In fact, Gary feels Culbertson's help and friendship have been invaluable.

Gary's life has not been free of racial twinges and bigotries experienced by minorities in spite of his artistic accomplishments, but the majority of people he deals with welcome him warmly to their cities and homes. Gary is rarely a stranger even in places he's not visited until he arrives with his exhibit at a museum. Junichi Shimizu, a promoter of Gary's show in Japan who had seen Twentieth-Century Dinosaurs at the Los Angeles County Museum, California, said to Gary in Tokyo, "How does it feel to be known before you get here?"

Media personalities and crews travel to Gary's shop in Hightstown, where they often deliberately extend their time to enjoy Gary's hospitality, the atmosphere of the shop in which fascinating sculptures are made, and the artist's stories and demonstrations of his work. Charles Osgood, then host of CBS-TV's "Good Morning America," spent the whole day with Gary as the crew filmed a particularly cohesive, imaginative segment for its viewers.

The crew members of ABC-TV's "Ripley's Believe It or Not!" followed Gary into the salvage yards off back roads and back to his shop to capture some of Gary's methods and ideas on film for the television series narrated by Jack Palance. They never seemed to mind the time—they told Gary they're not often sent on as interesting and meritorious an assignment as the one on Gary's sculpture.

The television show "Real People" had Gary on twice, the second time a result of his popularity among the show's staff and viewers.

A story and photographs of Twentieth-Century Dinosaurs were previewed in the Soviet Union under the auspices of the National Geographic Society. It was so well-received there, National Geographic World magazine decided to use the package as a cover story. A head shot of one of Gary's adorable birds graced the publication's September 1978 issue.

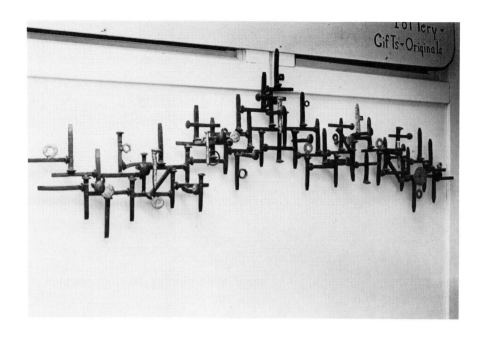

Museum directors also favor Gary's over other exhibits. Craig Black was director of Carnegie Museum of National History in 1982 when Gary's wholly original dinosaurs stood their ground among one of the world's most respected collections of real dinosaur skeletons. Black was to become director of the Los Angeles County Museum the next year, and he wanted Gary's show to be the first he produced there.

John B. Clark, director of The Bruce Museum in Connecticut, believes Gary's show is "a natural, especially considering the modern interest in dinosaurs and art" and that Gary is "a Renaissance character."

"As a scientist thrown into a more general field of working in a museum, I felt Twentieth-Century Dinosaurs would be perfect to exhibit and I knew it would attract crowds," Clark said. "This is not just a show, but a total educational program. A whole slew of activities were planned around the exhibit—that was the magic for us."

Clark said he had no trouble obtaining complete sponsorship for the show from the Junior League which is "interested in children as well as in the marriage of art and science," as Clark put it. "Because so many people were already familiar with Jim's work, the show sold itself. Certainly Jim's not in need of a heavy sell—he's so shy—as the people came out in droves to see the exhibit."

It is unusual for an individual, as opposed to corporations or other

"The common name first got my attention," James R. said. "My sister noticed a news story about a man with the same name as mine and sent me the clipping. I wrote Jim a letter expressing interest in his work, and later I took my family to his L.A. show and we introduced ourselves.

"Immediately, my kids and I were taken with the sculpture—it was a fantastic show," said James R., president of James R. Gary and Co., Ltd., Realtors and Estate Agents, of Woodland Hills, Ca. "We all had dinner and got to know each other. I'm involved in the arts and cultural society. The uniqueness of Jim's work struck me; I bought one of his 'Carburetor people' for myself and one for my friend Bert Boechmann, who owns Galpin Ford dealers in L.A."

James R. and Gary have maintained a relationship over the years, a social pleasure for both men highlighted by meeting at Gary's show at the California Academy of Sciences, San Francisco, and at the San Fernando Valley Cultural Foundation dinner. James R. said the organization is building an arts park in the Valley, which includes an amphitheater and a performing arts building with small theaters and offices. At the dinner, the sculptor was James R.'s guest and introduced to all the board members.

"He is a stellar-level, consummate artist in metal-working," said James R. of Gary. "His dinosaurs will undoubtedly be his primary and

organizations, to have created an entire show for a museum, and it is unorthodox for a museum to deal with an individual. Despite this, Clark said Gary's is a show with a human, creative sense unlike shows many museums typically mount.

"Jim's a very reasonable person to work with," said Clark, "and he has his feelings—as any artist would—about how his work should be installed. Actually, he *has* to be there to handle the pieces, especially the huge ones. It's a new experience for an institution to have Jim and his art, science and fun. Surely the result—the throng in to see the show—is also new to many institutions."

Gary realizes how his well-established reputation with museums continually bucks the gallery-representation system. "It may seem safer for a museum not to deal with an individual," said Gary. "Just think—if I didn't show up, plans for the whole exhibit would be destroyed." Never has there been an obstacle causing Gary to breach a contract with a museum: If a problem should arise, Gary will find a remedy with the same aplomb he uses to create. His friends attest to his ability to fix anything.

One friend thus described Gary's lessons to children: If life gives you lemons, make lemonade; there is the potential for beauty in everything. This friend, whose name is James R. Gary (hereafter referred to as James R., for clarity's sake), met Gary at the Los Angeles County Museum show.

best-known work. They capture the imagination and they are a positive, stimulating experience.

"But Jim works on several levels. Out of the mundane and normal by-products of life, he creates exciting work that everyone can interpret. To my children, Gretchen, Bryan and Andrew, the sculptures are 'awesome' and 'really radical.' Jim is very sensitive and spontaneous about what he does. He's very concerned about technical precision in his realism-and-surrealism that makes sense to me. So many of the things people put out today and stamp the word 'art' on it don't do much for me. But Jim's work is great."

James R. also has a table Gary made for his home. A Jim Gary poster hangs in his office.

Gary's popularity extends itself at times to people who are admirers, but who have odd ways of showing their admiration. During a three-day photo session for the National Geographic World magazine cover story, several of Gary's sculptures were placed in an Ocean Township, N.J., field. The photographers decided to wait for a change in the available light, and Gary's party left the field for a little while.

When they returned, the Dimetrodon, Alligator and Platosaurus were missing. Police conducted an intense but unproductive search.

"Two days later," Gary said, "I got a call from a man who said he had taken my sculptures to his barn because 'he just wanted to have them.' He must have heard about the police search and gotten scared.

Then he told me where I could pick up the sculptures as long as I promised not to press charges.

"I went to his place. He even helped me load them on my trailer. I was really happy to get the pieces back, and off I drove down Route 35.

"Suddenly, I was surrounded by police, who thought I had stolen the sculpture they'd been on the lookout for. After calling headquarters, they were finally convinced I was not the thief, but the sculptor. At least it was a comfort to me that the police were out there trying to help."

Dr. Frank H. Talbot, executive director of the California Academy of Sciences, described Gary's reaction to the theft of one of his butterflies during his exhibit there as considerably calm.

"He wasn't pleased with the theft," Talbot said, "but he was remarkable, even through some tension caused by children crawling all over his sculpture. One kid crashed on top of one of the animals made with a Volkswagen top, but it didn't seem to phase him. He is a charming, gentle person, nice to work with. His show was tremendously well-received."

It also caught the eye of film producer George Lucas, who shot several scenes in his movie "Howard the Duck" around Gary's dinosaurs. Gary himself appeared momentarily in the film, which was released in August 1986. Unfortunately, the film was not a box-office hit, but that Lucas told Gary he couldn't resist having the dinosaurs in some of the scenes was no less an accolade for the sculptor.

Dean Weldon, exhibit production chief of the California Academy, had worked closely with Gary to install the show and felt that much of Gary's charm was in his willingness to "get involved and get dirty."

"Gary is not an elitist artist in any way," Weldon said. "Some of the sculptures weigh a ton, but it didn't matter if he was in a suit and tie—he'd help you carry it in. We provided space—sort of an outdoor studio—where Jim welded, painted, finished things on site. The most charming aspect of this was that Jim is so hands-on. He even had a nice attitude about the children impacting the sculptures. While we had guards posted to try to keep the kids off, Jim realized the kids were so excited over the work and just had to express themselves."

"All of us were intrigued," Talbot added. "The pieces are extraordinarily realistic. But when you analyze them, you see how creative they are. Jim's mind is a brilliant and immense filing system. He must remember every spare part of all the old cars he's ever seen."

Gary's "filing system" seems as inexhaustible as his imagination, for which he is much in demand. Ann Berndt, chairman of the Belmont (a suburb of Boston) Schools Arts Council, bought a coloring book Gary had made to be sold at the museums in conjunction with his shows during his exhibit at the Boston Museum of Science. Ms. Berndt called Gary thereafter to ask him to visit several schools as artist-in-residence.

"I applied for a grant from the Belmont Savings Bank, which underwrote the entire project," Ms. Berndt said. "We've had a long tradition of bringing fine arts projects to the town, but this was so different. With his demonstrations (he worked very hard), talks and slide shows, he turned the town upside down."

Belmont's arts council members planned the activities around Gary's visit months in advance. They obtained recycled materials from the Boston Children's Museum and had the children create sculptures

with them in their art classes. These were on display in the Belmont Library and Gary was astounded. Video tapes of television shows Gary had been on were played, and Ms. Berndt said the council sold enough Twentieth-Century Dinosaurs T-shirts and coloring books to purchase one of Gary's birds for the library. The townspeople were so attracted to Gary that they competed to invite him to dinner, she said, and when he was totally booked for dinner, they'd invite him to breakfast and lunch.

"Belmont fell in love with him," said Ms. Berndt. "We had balloons with his name on them and we had a band. Jim said, 'This is the first time I had a band play for me.' Town officials, kids, all the school

people were there; it was a real old-fashioned, small-town bash.

"He's created such a sensation. The Museum of Science also invited him back as the special guest for their Dinamation show, and the Boston Globe, the Boston Herald and the Boston public television station, WGBH, featured him. It was a unifying experience for Belmont. Now a lot of other school systems want him to come there—Weston, Sudbury, and to Boston again for a week."

Ms. Berndt said the arts council is planning for Gary's next "residency" in Massachusetts.

Maryland's Montgomery County Public Schools have also chosen Gary's work to become part of the students' daily view. According to Stephen Steinhart, art program director for the county school system, Gary received a $28,000 commission—part of Montgomery County's "one-percent law"—to create dinosaur sculpture for the grounds of Jones Lane Elementary School, Rockville.

"Montgomery County (northwest of Washington, D.C.) has a large, affluent and educated population," Steinhart said, "One percent of the cost of public buildings is appropriated for works of art. In the past three years, 32 original works have been commissioned. Of the 50 or so entrants in the contest for the Jones Lane commission, Gary's dinosaurs—especially the Brontosaurus and Stegosaurus—attracted the judges. Not only does Gary's art have charm and originality, Gary is mild-mannered and pleasant (not all artists are) and he's easier to get along with than most artists."

By September 1987, Gary's sculpture will be on permanent display at the school for the children and for everyone. In addition, students can learn more about Gary as they develop their reading skills.

Vickie J. Woodruff, a Scott, Foresman editor, thought of Gary's sculpture when she was assigned to the non-fiction portions of *Running Free*, a reading text geared to the eight- or nine-year-old, average-to-good reader. The first printing of the book—50,000 copies —has been distributed to schools across the nation.

A combination of factors influenced Ms. Woodruff's selection. She wanted an interesting subject, she had seen the November 1983 issue of *Ranger Rick* magazine and heard about another feature story on Gary from a freelance writer, and she was delighted to find a black American artist to include in the text.

Few artists suit the pages of students' textbooks, Ms. Woodruff explained, "because the work of many artists is too esoteric and difficult to describe. You have to think of what the public wants children to read about. You want to show the role of artist on all levels.

"Jim Gary's work is artistic and accessible. You don't need a background in art to appreciate it, and if you do have a background in art, you appreciate it all the more," Ms. Woodruff said.

"It is very difficult to find a living artist with major credentials and recognition. Our association with Jim was very positive."

Sallie Luther, author of the *Ranger Rick* story on Gary and senior editor of the magazine, discovered the unique sculpture and its creator in much the same way Ms. Woodruff did. "One of our editors had seen Gary's exhibit at the Carnegie Museum, and we were sent some of the museum brochures in which Gary's work looked so intriguing," Ms. Luther said.

Ranger Rick, the flagship publication of the National Wildlife Federation—the world's largest private conservation organization— has a readership in the millions. It is primarily distributed in the United States, but it is available all over the world: in the USSR, Southeast Asia, the United Kingdom, Africa and most English-speaking nations.

"The interest in Jim Gary as a result of the story is second only to interest in Dr. Roy Mackal, the professor from the University of Chicago who is searching for the living dinosaur," Ms. Luther said. "We continually receive calls (and not only from kids) from people who ask, 'Where is Gary? Where is his studio?' The kids are fascinated to learn that Gary is a 'regular' guy who turns junkyard stuff into wonderful creations. He is a role model and a foremost modern sculptor."

The *Ranger Rick* article was not the first such attention Gary had received; his art steals the show as a matter of record since Gary began exhibiting in the sidewalk and shopping-mall events. Even if a museum displays other related dinosaur items (including Dinamation and the paintings of Charles Knight), it is Gary's sculpture that magnetizes the media and the museum visitors and conjures up indomitable enthusiasm.

When Gary participated in an Equitable Life Assurance Society art show in New York, the firm's executives couldn't help but notice the public favor toward his pieces. Frank Macri, president of Equitable's Communications Design Group division, said Gary's work, "as one component of a larger show, drew such attention that I sought him out, and we eventually decided to do a one-man show.

"Jim's work had strength, diversity and excitement—it didn't need to be tempered by the work of others," Macri said. "For Equitable to offer a one-man show was uncommon, but Jim is an achiever and an inspiration." Even blacks employed by Equitable in all capacities expressed their pride at having a black artist's work on display, Macri told Gary.

Macri added that one of the top executives, very conservative and well-versed in the arts, bought a Gary original for his office as a focal point. Such a purchase seemed incongruous with this particular man's personality, Macri said, but it illustrated that Gary's was one of the most imaginative and well-attended exhibits in the firm's art gallery.

Television cameras caught the flatbed trailer as it pulled up in front of the Equitable building. "The sculpture of Jim Gary is an adventure," Macri said, "You never know where it will lead."

It has led everywhere from *The Book of Knowledge Annual 1985*, in which the pages and photographs on Gary were conceived by executive editor Fern L. Mamberg after reading *Ranger Rick*, to Tokyo in May 1984 just as the cherry-blossom season came to an end.

After a 14-hour flight, Gary arrived in Japan. He had barely looked around when he was whisked into a meeting to settle some business matters for the Twentieth Century Dinosaurs exhibit and then to a 6 a.m. taping of a popular "Good Morning Japan"-type show.

On the "set," the dinosaurs had been arranged and the host— apparently a facile conversationalist and something of a comedian— was about to introduce Gary as their creator. For this show, a local welder/mechanic had been commissioned to forge a Gary dinosaur, and the piece he'd put together was also to be shown and explained.

At first, Gary was perturbed to see an imitation of his work, executed without his knowledge or consent. But the piece was of no consequence, for the mechanic had to use ugly poles to keep the piece—a lame Tyrannosaurus—standing upright.

The show was aired at seven. Gary ate breakfast with several people involved in the exhibit at Takashimaya's People's Museum, and was then embraced by the tense production period of the installation.

Hundreds of thousands of people came to see the exhibit, which was thoughtfully and dramatically designed and could not have been

ignored. The Asahi newspaper, a major daily publication, covered the event and whimsical posters announcing its whereabouts and duration were placed even in the immaculate subway train cars that traveled throughout Tokyo and to other cities.

The popularity of the exhibit led to plans for a sculpture park designed around Gary's dinosaurs by Ko Creations, an art/advertising company based in Tokyo.

The Japanese treated Gary in a royal fashion until his visit was to end, on May Day when there were magnificent parades through the city streets.

It had been an extraordinary trip, the first time Gary took his show off the North American continent to a foreign land. His Japanese hosts provided a whirlwind of activity, both related to the exhibit and intimate tours of the different wards of the world's largest city. Clearly, Gary's art travels well and transcends cultures. It is a very human art.

As Twentieth-Century Dinosaurs, along with his other sculptures, continue to mark their miles around the globe, so will Gary's art become even more alive, imaginative and adventurous than people have described until now. The only real hurdles will arise in what Gary expects of himself as an artist, as a perfectionist. His own standards for the quality of his work emerged very early in his life, and these he could not help but impart to others. He would work and re-work a piece until it was honed to its best possible form.

When he taught people to weld, he was an incorrigible taskmaster. He recounted taking one woman's welded piece and hurling it across his shop. It fell to pieces, and the woman began to cry. Then he threw one of his pieces down; it remained intact, and that was the crux of the lesson.

Gary once said, in a rare moment of thinking aloud, "My greatest fear is that something will fall apart." But so fierce and persistent is his technique that it has not and will not.

Gary's art already has a permanent place in the modern world, a fine-welded chain, if you will, that has many more miles to go before its links meet end to end.

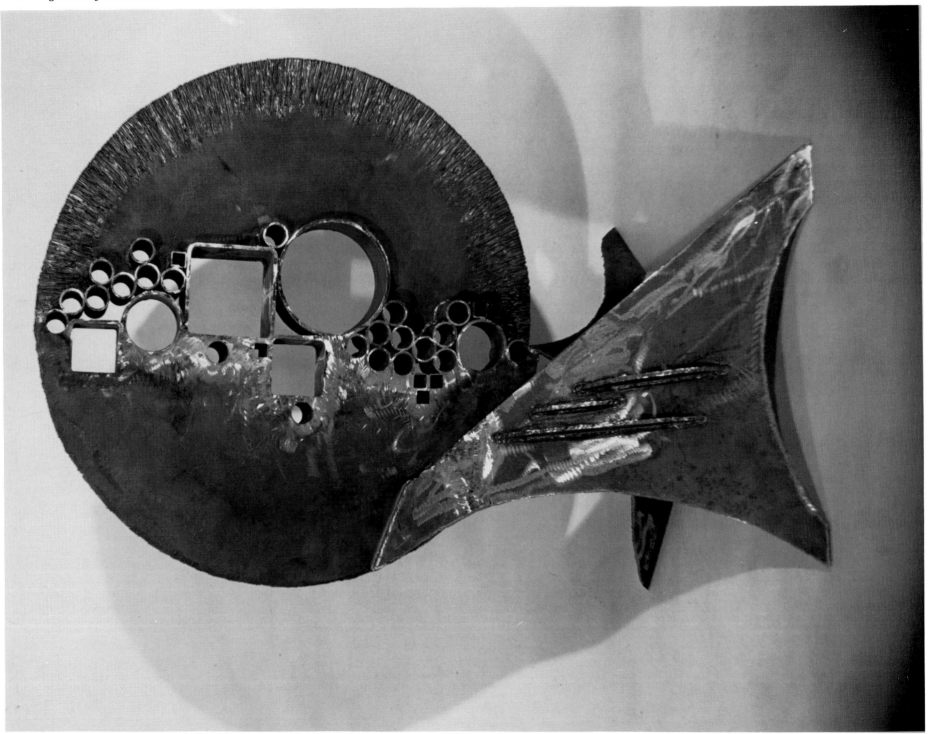

Catalogue of Works

1. Dimetrodon	13′ x 5′	
2. Stegosaurus	25′ x 7′	
3. Alligator	13′ x 2′	
4. Pteranodon	12′ x 18′ (wing span)	
5. Brontosaurus	42′ x 14′	
6. Brontosaurus	32′ x 11′	
7. Tyrannosaurus rex	24′ x 12′	
8. Fossil (relief)	25′	
9. Turtle	12′ x 3′	
10. Ankylosaurus	14′ x 4′	
11. Platosaurus	15′ x 9′	
12. Duck-Billed	20′ x 13′	
13. Eryops	10′ x 2′	
14. Allosaurus	20′ x 5½′	
15. Plesiosaurus	30′ x 14′	
16. Deinonyhus	9′ x 5′	
17. Dimetrodon Fossil		
18. Large Red Bird	7′	
19. Yellow Ostrich	7½′	
20. Red Ostrich	7′	
21. Yellow Bird	4′	
22. Duck	4′	
23. Planter Bird	3½′	
24. Planter Bird	7′	
25. Ant	2′ x 5′	
26. Blue Spider Bug		
27. Purple Bug		
28. Red Short Snout Bug		
29. Green Bug		
30. Yellow Spider Bug		
31. Flowers		
32. Carburetor People		
33. Butterfly (magazine rack)		
34. Butterflies		
35. Coffee Table with glass (round)		
Oval 2x5		
Desk		
36. Glass Nude		
37. Wednesday We Took Off		
38. Spring Maid		
39. Universal Woman		
40. Cube Torso		
41. Brass Bitch		
42. Wall Relief Floral		

43. Abstract Circles	
44. Spring Neck Birds	
45. Butterfly (Various colors, no glass)	
46. Butterfly (Various colors, with glass)	
47. Dragonfly (without glass)	
48. Dragonfly (with glass)	
49. Brass fish with glass	
50. Wall Relief Abstract Enamel	
51. Screen	
52. Tin Man	
53. XAX	
54. Tranquil	
55. Cat-O-Nine Tails	
56. Standing Flower with Butterfly	
57. Radio	
58. Sun Dial	
59. Courting Seat	
60. Chicken	
61. Abstract (circles)	
62. Abstract (triangles)	
63. Road Runner	
64. Bicentennial Bird	
65. '76 Bird	
66. Signs of the Times	
67. Michelob Wreath	
68. Space Needle	
69. Hanging Liquor Cabinet	
70. Sunburst	
71. Tree (relief)	
72. Standing Abstract Tree	
73. Long stemmed roses	
74. Street Scene	
75. Gear Train	
76. Candle Holder	
77. Coil Lamp	
78. Abstract Lamp	
79. Menorah	
80. Brotherhood Through the Arts	10′
81. Lollipop	4′
82. Stained Glass Lady	5′
83. The Coming of Spring	

SPECIAL DELIVERY!

BUG OFF, BLUMBURTT!

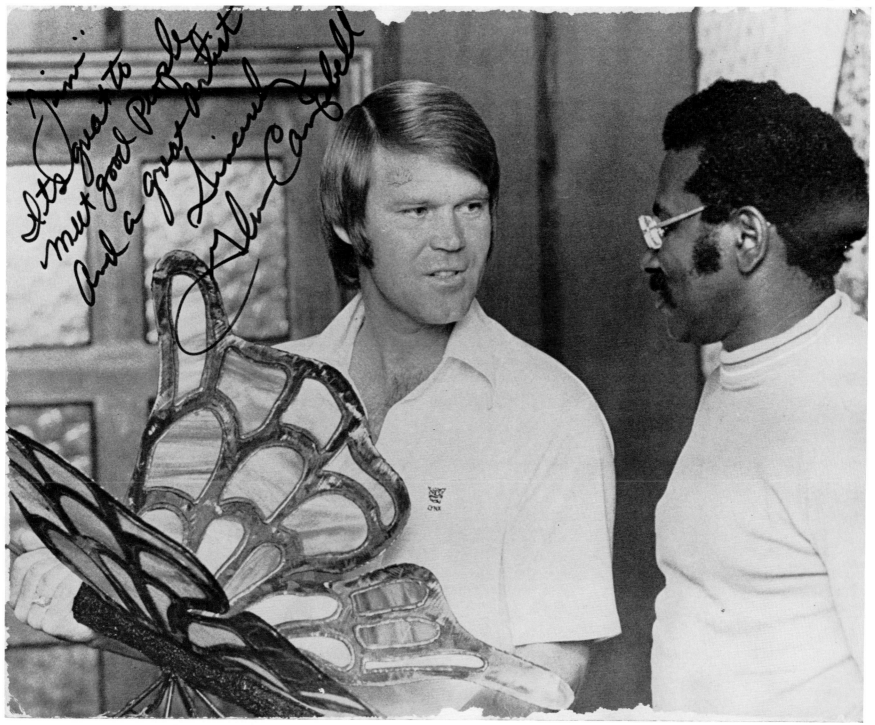

Exhibitions

1. Ford Foundation National Industrial Arts Show—Madison Square Garden, N.Y., N.Y., First & Third Place 1969
2. Garden State Art Center, Holmdel, N.J., July 1970, 1971
3. Asbury Park Society Fine Arts—Asbury Park, N.J., First Place Artists and People's Choice, 1970, One-man Show 1971
4. A Salute to Black Artists, New Jersey State Museum, Trenton, N.J. 1972
5. Smith-Mason Gallery of Art, Black Artists 1971, Washington D.C., First Place Nationals, in conjunction with the Smithsonian Institution 1971
6. Red Bank Art Show, Red Bank, N.J., First Place 1972, 1973
7. Montclair Art Association Art Show, Montclair, N.J., First Place 1973
8. American Iron & Steel Institute—New York, N.Y., Participant 1973
9. N.J. Teen Arts Festival, State Museum Cultural Center, Trenton, N.J., sponsored by Department of Education 1973, 1974 and other years
10. Franklin Lakes Arts Council, Franklin Lakes, N.J., Best in Show, 1972, First Place, 1973, 1974
11. One-man Show, Garden State Art Center, Holmdel, N.J, July, 1973
12. One-man Show, Rutgers University, Newark, N.J., December, 1974
13. Atlantic City Boardwalk Art Show, Atlantic City, N.J., 1st Place, 1976, 1st Place, 1975, Best in Show 1974
14. Courtyard Gallery, Birmingham, Ala. 1974
15. National Audubon Society, New York, N.Y., 1974
16. National Academy of Design, New York, N.Y., 1974
17. Showcase, Monmouth County Council of the Arts, West Long Branch, N.J. 1975
18. Lakewood High School, Lakewood, N.J., grant by N.J. Council on the Arts, 1975
19. Greater New York Automobile Show, New York, N.Y., 1975, 1976
20. One-man Show, Rutgers University, New Brunswick, N.J., February 1975
21. One-man Show, Middlesex Community College, Edison, N.J., April, 1975
22. Benedict Gallery, Madison, N.J., 1975
23. One-man Show, Staten Island Zoological Society, Staten Island, N.Y., September 1975
24. Menlo Park Art Show, Edison, N.J.
25. Princeton Shoppers Mall Art Show, Princeton, N.J.
26. Monmouth Mall Art Show, Eatontown, N.J.
27. Mid-State Mall Art Show, East Brunswick, N.J.
28. Cherry Hill Mall Art Show, Cherry Hill, N.J., April 1978
29. Perimeter Mall Art Show, Atlanta, Ga.
30. Yoshameti Mall Art Show, Yoshameti, Pa.
31. Woodbridge Center Art Show, Woodbridge, N.J.
32. Manhasset Mall Art Show, Manhasset, N.J.
33. Livingston Mall Art Show, Livingston, N.J.
34. Willowbrook Mall Art Show, Wayne, N.J.
35. Moorestown Mall Art Show, Moorestown, N.J.
36. University of Atlanta, Birmingham, Ala.
37. Douglass College, New Brunswick, N.J.
38. Brookdale Community College, Lincroft, N.J.
39. Monmouth College, West Long Branch, N.J.
40. Middlesex Community College, Edison, N.J.
41. N.J. Association for Retarded Children, Red Bank, N.J.
42. Stewart Country Day School, Princeton, N.J.
43. St. John Delbarton School, Morristown, N.J.
44. Hilltop Academy, Holmdel, N.J.
45. Grier School, Tyrone, Pa.
46. Middlesex Technical School, East Brunswick, N.J.
47. Long Branch Public School, Long Branch, N.J.
48. Navesink School, Fair Haven, N.J.
49. Elberon School, Elberon, N.J.
50. Colts Neck School, Colts Neck, N.J.
51. Lincroft School, Lincroft, N.J.
52. Nutswamp School, Middletown, N.J.
53. Oakhurst Library, Oakhurst, N.J.
54. Monmouth County Library, Eastern Branch, Shrewsbury, N.J.
55. Middletown Library, Middletown, N.J.
56. Fairlawn Library, Fairlawn, N.J.
57. Monmouth County YMCA, Community Centers, Womens Clubs, Art Clubs
58. YMHA, Asbury Park & Perth Amboy, N.J.
59. Village Woman's Club, Middletown, N.J.
60. Bell Labs Art Club, Holmdel, N.J.
61. Brandeis University National Woman's Committee, North Brunswick, N.J.
62. Woman's Club of New Shrewsbury, Shrewsbury, N.J.
63. ''Images in Metal,'' The Equitable Gallery, New York, N.Y. May 1977
64. University of Pittsburgh, Pa., October 1977
65. Ithaca College, Ithaca, N.Y., April 1977 and April 1976
66. University of Delaware, Newark, Del., September 1976
67. Bergen County Community Museum, Newark, N.J., April, 1976
68. Monmouth Mall, Eatontown, N.J., August 1976

69. Middlesex Community College, 1976 and 1975
70. Monmouth Museum, Lincroft, N.J., 1976, 1978
71. Garden State Art Center, Holmdel, N.J.
72. Cloister Museum, The Cloisters, New York, N.Y.
73. Pennsylvania Auto & Trucking Salvage Association, Harrisburg, Pa.
74. Guest Artist, Sculpture League of New York, February, 1977 and November, 1977
75. National Sculpture Society, The Equitable Gallery, January, 1977
76. "The Spirit in Art," St. John's Church, Newark, N.J., December 1977
77. 1st Biennal New Jersey Artists, Newark Museum, N.J. October–December 1977
78. Western Electric Co., Hopewell, N.J.
79. Morris Museum of Arts & Sciences, Convent, N.J., July 3–August 15 1979
80. Maraback Museum, Willingboro, N.J.
81. College of Mount St. Vincent & Manhattan College, N.Y.
82. Trenton State College, Trenton, N.J.
83. N.J. College of Medicine, Newark, N.J.
84. Florida A & M University, Tallahassee, Fla., April 1978
85. The Academy of Natural Sciences, Philadelphia, Pa., January 27–April 8, 1979
86. The Bruce Museum, Greenwich, Conn., September–October 1979
87. The Children's Museum, Indianapolis, Ind., January 12–March 9, 1980
88. Capital Children's Museum, Washington, D.C., April–August 1980
89. Cranbrook Institute, Detroit, Mich., June–July 1980
90. The Equitable Gallery, Equitable Life Assurance Society, New York, N.Y., August 18–29, 1980
91. Bell Laboratories, Holmdel, N.J., August 1981. This show set attendance records throughout the Bell System for art exhibits.
92. Poricy Park, Middleton, N.J., October 1981
93. Charleston Museum, Charleston, S.C., April–May 1981. This exhibit opened the new museum and was viewed by international dignitaries.
94. Memphis Pink Palace Museum, Memphis, Tenn., January 30–April 4, 1982
95. Carnegie Museum of Natural History, Carnegie Institute, Pittsburgh, Pa., April 17–May 30, 1982
96. Amarillo Discovery Center, Amarillo, Texas, July 1–September 17, 1982

97. Los Angeles County Museum of Natural History, Los Angeles, Calif., January 28–May 1, 1983
98. The Milwaukee Public Museum, Milwaukee, Wis., May 1984
99. Anniston Museum of Natural History, Anniston, Ala., September 15–October 21, 1984
100. Field Museum of Natural History, Chicago, Ill., October 1984
101. Boston Museum of Science, Boston, Mass., November 1984–February 1985
102. People's Museum, Takashimaya, Tamagawa Ward, Tokyo, Japan, April–May 1984, to a six-month tour to other locations in Japan.

103. Denver Museum of Natural History, Denver, Colo. June–
104. California Academy of Sciences, San Francisco, Calif., June 27–November 10, 1985
105. Pacific Science Center, Seattle, Wash., February 1–March 2, 1986
106. Sacramento Science Center, Sacramento, Calif.
107. St. Louis Science Center, St. Louis, Mo., April 5–June 29, 1986.
108. On permanent display in "Discovering Dinosaurs" hall, The Academy of Natural Sciences, Philadelphia, Pa., since December 31, 1985.
109. Madison Park High School, Roxbury, Mass., September 1986.

Collectors

1. AT&T
2. Bell Laboratories, Holmdel Township, N.J.
3. Glen Campbell
4. Equitable Life Assurance Society, New York, N.Y.
5. Bulova
6. Riverview Medical Center, Red Bank, N.J.
7. Rutgers, The State University, New Brunswick, N.J.
8. Stuart Leven, Top of the Park, New York, N.Y.
9. Children's Museum, Indianapolis, Ind.
10. The Bruce Museum, Greenwich, Conn.
11. Johnson & Johnson, Princeton, N.J.
12. Ramco Steel Corporation, Newark, N.J.
13. Walter Reade Theaters, Middletown and Asbury Park, N.J.
14. Fry & Welch Associates, P.E., Washington, D.C.
15. Milliman & Robertson, Inc., New York, N.Y.
16. Monmouth Mall, Eatontown, N.J.
17. Garden State Rehabilitation Hospital, Toms River, N.J.
18. A.G.S. Computer Institute, Woodbridge, N.J.
19. Greater New York Automobile Show
20. Neptune Municipal Building, Neptune, N.J.
21. Howell Jewish Community Center, Howell Township, N.J.
22. RBT Inc., Greenwich, Conn.
23. Prestige Motors, Paramus, N.J.
24. Smith Cadillac, Elizabeth, N.J.
25. Ambridge Auto, Inc., Ambridge, Pa.
26. Automobile Dismantlers Association of U.S.
27. Lane Robbins School
28. Nancy Holland
29. Marilyn Nasta
30. Stuart Duncan, Princeton, N.J.
31. Morton Weiss, Morristown, Pa.
32. E. Jaig, Union City, N.J.
33. Joseph Pellegrino, Lowell, Mass.
34. William and Joyce Michaelson, South Orange, N.J.
35. Irwin and Betsy Vogel, Red Bank, N.J.
36. Leonard Sadow, New York, N.Y.
37. St. Benedict's Church, Holmdel Township, N.J.
38. Morton Baumgarten, Woodbridge, N.J.
39. Ocean City National Bank, Bay Head, N.J.
40. Boston Museum of Sciences, Boston, Mass.
41. Stuart Country Day School, Princeton, N.J.
42. Jerrel Office Building, Shrewsbury, N.J.
43. Town Chevrolet, Middletown, N.J.
44. Phillipsburg Public Library, Phillipsburg, N.J.
45. James and Arlene Berg, Colts Neck, N.J.
46. Daniel and Susan Roth, Holmdel Township, N.J.
47. Stephen Schwartz, Ridgefield, Conn.
48. Ronald Gruber, Holmdel Township, N.J.
49. Louis A. deFuria, Livingston, N.J.
50. Daniel J. McCarthy, New York, N.Y.
51. Dr. and Mrs. Elliot Altman, Freehold, N.J.
52. Mr. and Mrs. J.R. Lutz, Birmingham, Mich.
53. Ken and Kate Baynes, Gloucestershire, England
54. William and Cynthia Nixon, Birmingham, Mich.
55. David Littmann, Bloomfield Hills, Mich.
56. Dagmar Dockey
57. Robert Carter
58. Joan Cameron
59. Dickstein Associates, Inc.
60. Carol Michaels
61. Celeste Roberts
62. Nassau Welding
63. Middlesex Community College
64. John and Tova Navarra, Howell Township, N.J.
65. William and Carol East, Birmingham, Ala.
66. Mr. and Mrs. John Reece
67. Mr. and Mrs. Edward R. Pompadur
68. James R. Gary and Co. Ltd. Realtors, Woodland Hills, Ca.
69. Bert Boeckmann, Galpin Ford, Inc., Los Angeles, Ca.
70. David Vowell, Los Angeles, Ca.
71. Elisa N. Treadwell, Phoenix, N.Y.
72. Max and Lillian Houss, Colts Neck, N.J.
73. Dr. and Mrs. Seymour M. Gross

Bibliography: Published Sources on Gary

The following is only a partial list, due to the fact that many clipping services failed to identify (or identify clearly) the publication in which an item appeared. Also, many articles on Jim Gary have been clipped by appreciative spectators throughout the country and sent to Gary minus the name and date of the publication. Others were destroyed by fire.

Many of these served as sources of information for the text of this book.

1. *The Daily Register,* Shrewsbury, N.J.,1971, Oct. 4, 1972, Sept. 10, 1975, 1978, 1981, 1985
2. *The Daily News* (centerfold), New York, N.Y., Dec. 9, 1974, Jan. 11, 1977
3. *Ebony,* New York, N.Y., and Chicago, Ill., Oct. 1976
4. *Small World,* Englewood, N.J., Sept. 1976
5. *New York Times,* New York, N.Y., Jan., April 2, 1976, June 1976; July 15, 1979
6. *The Herald Tribune,* Paris, France (front page), April 19, 1976
7. *News Parade,* May 5, 1976
8. *Senior Weekly,* Dec. 1, 1976
9. *New Jersey Music & Arts,* Chatham, N.J., April 1974, Nov. 1975; Jan. 1978
10. *The Sunday Advisor,* Middletown, N.J., Nov. 14, 1976
11. *Greater New York Automobile Show* magazine, New York, N.Y., 1976
12. *Know Your World,* Feb. 2, 1977
13. *Weekly Reader News Hunt,* Middletown, Conn., *Feb. 2, 1977*
14. *Monmouth,* Sunday Magazine, Jan. 21, 1977 *(The Sunday Register,* Shrewsbury, N.J.)
15. *Associated Press,* Photo Essay, Jan. 1977
16. *Equinews,* Equitable Life Assurance Society, New York, N.Y., 1977
17. *Asbury Park Press,* Neptune, N.J., 1976, 1979, 1980, 1983, 1984, Aug. 8, 1985
18. *Colts Neck Newsletter,* Colts Neck, N.J., 1978
19. *National Geographic World,* (cover story), Washington, D.C., Sept. 1978
20. *New Jersey Monthly,* Morristown, N.J., May 1978
21. *The Mini-Page,* Feb. 1978
22. *The Quadrangle,* 1978
23. *The Tallahassee Democrat,* Tallahassee, Fla., April 20, 1978
24. *New York Times,* (New Jersey Section cover), New York, N.Y., May 30, 1979; Sept. 22, 1979
25. *Greenwich Times,* Sept. 1979
26. *The Star,* Tarrytown, N.Y., Feb. 20, 1979
27. International Wire Services (UPI and AP), Jan. 1979
28. *The Explorer,* The Bruce Museum, Greenwich, Conn., Fall 1979
29. Bowmar/Noble *Special People Reading Comprehension Series,* Los Angeles, Calif., Dec. 1979
30. *Natural History Museum Directory,* Sept. 1979
31. *Scholastic Magazine,* Fall 1979
32. *Jet* magazine, Chicago, Ill., March 1979
33. *Today* magazine, Feb. 1979
34. *Tech Center News, The Monday Morning Sun,* 1980
35. *The Independent,* Rural Hall, N.C., Sept. 11, 1980
36. *Winston-Salem Chronicle,* Winston-Salem, N.C., Sept. 13, 1980
37. *Scholastic News Ranger* (Teachers' Edition), New York, N.Y., April 1980
38. AP Wire Service article, Summer 1980
39. *Freehold Press* (several articles) 1980
40. *MuseumScope,* Memphis, Tenn., Dec. 1981
41. *Steel '81,* American Iron and Steel Institute, Washington, D.C., (Spring) 1981
42. *Detroit Free Press,* Detroit, Ill., July 1981
43. *American Welding Journal,* Miami, Fla., Fall 1981
44. *Games* magazine, New York, N.Y., Jan./Feb. 1981
45. *Diversion,* magazine, Fall 1981
46. *Pittsburgh Post-Gazette,* editorial, April 1982; *Pittsburgh Post-Gazette Weekend Magazine,* Pittsburgh, Pa., April 1982
47. *The Daily News* (Pa.), April 1982
48. *Daily Tribune* (Pa.), April 16, 20, 1982
49. *The Pittsburgh Press Sunday Roto Magazine,* Pittsburgh, Pa., April 1982
50. *Market Square of Pittsburgh,* Pittsburgh, Pa., April 14, 1982
51. *The Daily News* (Ca.), Jan. 1983
52. *Los Angeles Times,* Jack Smith editorial, Los Angeles, Calif., April 1983
53. *The Christian Science Monitor,* April 1983
54. *The Home News,* New Brunswick, N.J., 1983
55. *VW & Porsche* magazine, Los Angeles, Calif., Oct. 1983
56. *Terra,* Los Angeles County Museum of Natural History, Los Angeles, Calif., 1983
57. *Ranger Rick,* Washington, D.C., Nov. 1983
58. *Porsche-Audi Magazine*
59. *Ford Times,* March 1983
60. *AutoWeek,* Detroit, Mich., Feb. 1983
61. *San Gabriel Valley Daily Tribune Weekender,* April 1983
62. *County of Los Angeles Digest,* March 1983
63. *Indianapolis News,* Indianapolis, Ind., 1980

64. *Time Off* (cover story), *Windsor-Hights Herald/Princeton Packet*, Princeton, N.J., Jan. 13, 1984

65. *Milwaukee Courier*, Milwaukee, Wis., 1984

66. *Key* (Milwaukee), May 1984

67. *South Side Spirit*, 1984 (Milwaukee)

68. *Community Journal*, 1984 (Milwaukee)

69. *The Ave News*, 1984 (Milwaukee)

70. *The Sentinel*, Winston-Salem, N.C., Aug. 25, 1980; Sept. 11, 1980, Sept. 29, 1980, Oct. 6, 1980

71. *Sentinel*, Milwaukee, Wis., 1984

72. *The Birmingham News*, Birmingham, Ala., Sept. 1984

73. *The Anniston Star*, Anniston, Ala., Sept. 1984

74. *Lore*, Milwaukee Public Museum, Milwaukee, Wis., Spring 1984

75. *Asahi Evening News*, Tokyo, Japan, April 1984

76. *Community Paper Tamagawa*, Tokyo, Japan, April 1984

77. *The Milwaukee Journal*, Milwaukee, Wis., 1984

78. *USA Today*, Arlington, Va., and Washington, D.C., Oct. 4, 1984

79. *The Cranbury Press*, Dec. 19, 1984, Jan. 11, 1984

80. *The Cincinnati Enquirer*, Cincinnati, Ohio

81. *Windsor-Hights Herald* (Lifestyle cover), Dec. 19, 1984

82. *Mobil Motorist*, Fall 1984

83. *The Electric Company Magazine* (Children's Television Workshop)

84. *The New Book Of Knowledge Annual*, Grolier, Inc., Danbury, Conn., 1985

85. *The Record*, Hackensack, N.J., April 8, 1985

86. *Weekly Reader*, Middletown, Conn., Aug. 10, 1979

87. *Scholastic News*, New York, N.Y., March 1985

88. *Disney's Wonderful World of Knowledge Yearbook*, Grolier, Inc., Danbury, Conn., 1985

89. *Syracuse Herald-Journal*, Jan. 24, 1977; *Daytona Beach Morning Journal*, Jan. 24, 1977; *The Journal-News* (N.Y.), Jan. 24, 1977; *The Dallas Morning News*, Jan. 24, 1977; *The Wichita Eagle*, Feb. 15, 1977; (all AP stories, see note #15)

90. *Sculpture* (National Sculpture Review), New York, N.Y., Summer 1976

91. *The Boston Phoenix*, Boston, Mass., Feb. 5, 1985

92. Cranberry World, *Anniversary Festival of Music and Arts*, 1980

93. *Scholastic News*, New York, N.Y., Jan. 11, 1985

94. *Scholastic News Trails*, New York, N.Y., Jan. 10, 1980

95. *Yours for the Learning* (Carnegie Museum/Carnegie Institute), Pittsburgh, Pa., Spring 1982

96. *Allison Forge Corporation* magazine, 1985

97. Bell, Kathleen L., Paden, Frances Freeman, and Schaffrath, Susan Duffy, *Building English Skills*, McDougal, Littell & Co., Evanston, Ill., 1980

98. "Cayugan," Ithaca College Yearbook, Ithaca, N.Y., Volume 2, 1976.

99. "Artisan 78," publication of 4th Annual Harvest Crafts Festival, Nassau Coliseum, Uniondale, N.Y., Nov. 17, 18, 19, 1978

100. *The Jersey Journal*, Jersey City, N.J., June 19, 1973, Jan. 23, 1976

101. *The News Tribune*, Woodbridge, N.J., Feb. 8, 1974

102. *Sunday News*, (New York), Dec. 31, 1972

103. "Quo Vadis," Middlesex County College, Edison, N.J., April 25, 1975

104. "Spectrum," *The Star-Ledger*, Newark, N.J., Oct. 8, 1972; *The Star-Ledger*, Sept. 25, 1972; April 3, 1972; May 23, 1972; Aug. 10, 1976

105. *San Francisco Chronicle*, San Francisco, Calif., July 6, 1985

106. Garden State Rehabilitation Hospital, Toms River, N.J., brochure

107. *Motor Trend*, Los Angeles, Calif., Feb. 1986

108. *Parents' Monthly*, Sacramento, Calif.

109. *Scholastic News Pilot*, Teachers' Edition, New York, N.Y., Nov. 29, 1979

110. *New Center News*, Detroit (Mich.), June 9, 1980

111. *Daily Tribune*, Monroeville, Pa., April 16, 1982

112. *Evening Standard*, Uniontown, Pa., April 16, 1982

113. *McKees Rocks Gazette*, McKees Rocks, Pa., April 7, 1982

114. *Southwest Journal*, Pittsburgh, Pa., April 14, 1982

115. *The Tribune-Democrat Trend*, Pittsburgh, Pa., April 11, 1982

116. *The Tribune-Review*, Pittsburgh, Pa., April 4, 1982

117. *La Dolce Vita*, North Pittsburgh, Pa., April 19, 1982

118. *Winston-Salem Journal*, Winston-Salem, N.C., Sept. 9, 1980

119. *St. Louis Post-Dispatch*, St. Louis, Mo., April 3, 1986

120. "Museum Lines," Sacramento Science Center and Junior Museum, Sacramento, Calif., Nov. 1985

121. *EA View*, May 1980 (General Motors trade publishers)

122. *Watertown Press*, Watertown, Massachusetts, Dec. 27, 1984, Jan. 24, 1985

123. *Rockingham Gazette*, Exeter, N.H., Dec. 1984

124. *Lakes Region Trader*, Laconia, N.H., Jan. 2, 1985

125. *Patriot Ledger*, Quincy, Mass., Jan. 8, 1985

126. *Waterbury American*, Waterbury, Conn., Feb. 1, 1985

127. *The Enterprise*, Brockton, Mass., Feb. 5, 1985

128. *Middlesex News*, Framingham, Mass., Jan. 25, 1985

129. *The Independent,* Woonsocket, R.I., Jan. 1985
130. *Morning Union,* Springfield, Mass., Jan. 30, 1985
131. *Rockland Standard,* Rockland, Mass., Jan. 23, 1985
132. *Mansfield News,* Mansfield, Mass., Jan. 10, 1985
133. *Transcript Telegram,* Holyoke, Mass., Jan. 17, 1985
134. *Swampscott Reporter,* Marblehead, Mass., Jan. 10, 1985
135. *Canton Journal,* Canton, Mass., Dec. 28, 1984
136. *Clinton Daily Item,* Clinton, Mass., April 25, 1985
137. *Haverhill Gazette,* Haverhill, Mass., Jan. 10, 1985
138. *Dorchester Argus Citizen,* Hyde Park, Mass., Jan. 1985
139. *Sunday Republican,* Springfield, Mass., Jan. 20, 1985
140. *Fitchburg Leominster Sentinal & Enterprise,* Fitchburg, Mass., Jan. 7, 1985
141. *New England Entertainment Digest,* Marshfield, Mass., Jan. 25, 1985
142. *Daily News,* Newburyport, Mass., Jan. 24, 1985
143. *East Bridgewater Citizen,* Stoughton, Mass., Jan. 1985
144. *Carriage News,* South Boston, Mass., Jan. 1985
145. *Daily Times & Chronicle,* Reading, Mass., Jan. 10, 1985
146. *Journal Tribune,* Biddeford, Maine, Jan. 25, 1985 (UPI)
147. *The Evening Citizen,* Laconia, N.H., Jan. 29, 1985
148. *Cape Cod Times,* Hyannis, Mass., Jan. 30, 1985
149. *The Robb Report,* The Magazine for Connoisseurs, Acton, Mass., Dec. 1986
150. *Gaslines,* trade publication of Oxyco, Cannon Press, Zimbabwe, Africa, Vol. 2, 1982
151. *Art Business News,* Stamford, Conn., Nov. 1986
152. *Britt,* magazine of Britt Airways, Inc., September/October 1985
153. *The Boston Herald,* Boston, Mass., Sept. 25, 1986
154. *"Macy's California"* (cover and inside cover), advertising supplement to the *Examiner/Chronical, San Jose Mercury News, The Tribune, Sacramento Bee, Stockton Record, Monterey Peninsula Herald, Nevada State Journal/Reno Gazette, Conta Costa Times, Daily Review, Argus, Enterprise, Tri-Valley Herald and Enterprise, Santa Rosa Press Democrat, Modesto Bee, Fresno Bee, Fairfield Daily Republic, Vallejo Times, Vacaville Reporter, Napa Register, and the Marin Independent,* Aug. 25, 1985
155. *Welt am Sonntag,* "Lebens, Art", Dec. 7, 1986, Nr. 49, Seite 54. (In German)
156. *The Sunday Home News,* (page one) New Brunswick, N.J., May 17, 1970
157. *Cranbrook Institute of Science Annual Report,* Bloomfield Hills, Mich., 1979–80
158. *Gilpinite,* Yearbook of Gilpin County School, Black Hawk, Colo., 1985.

Eleven Alive & Channel 2 News, Pittsburgh, Pa., Sept. 1977
Eyewitness News Special New York, September 1976
WPIX News, New York, Jan. 1977
Eyewitness News, Wilmington, Del. September 1976
New Jersey Public Broadcasting (Channel 52, 58, & 13)
    July 1976
Captain Kangaroo, CBS, N.Y. January 1978
To Tell The Truth, CBS, 1977
Wonderama, WNEW, N.Y., Nov. 1976
Midday Live, WNEW, N.Y., April 1976
Today Show, N.Y., NBC
Philadelphia Today Show, Phila., Pa.
Cable TV (Phila.) Education Series presented by the
    New Jersey State Museum Magic Muse
Talk Show of Birmingham, Alabama
Real People
That's Incredible!
Good Morning America
CNN
Dinosaur!
Ripley's Believe It or Not
The Joe Franklin Show

NATIONAL GEOGRAPHIC

world

SEPTEMBER 1978

Monkeys in Danger
Police Training
Robots
Sailboat Race

The Children's Museum   30th & Meridian   Indianapolis, Indiana 46208   317-924-5431

Mildred S. Compton, Director

March 17, 1980

Jim Gary
Iron Butterfly Studio
Eight Broad Street
Red Bank, New Jersey 07701

Dear Jim:

How tremendous it has been to have your "Twentieth Century
Dinosaur" exhibit from January 12 to March 9, 1980 at The
Children's Museum. It is the first exhibition which we
have had for which we received universally excellent comments from all segments of our visitors. The appeal is
certainly very natural for children and adults alike. I
noticed in the comments on the registration book at the
exhibit that individuals· were generally expressing "how
neat," "how imaginative you must be" and "I think the museum should have more material like this in the future."

As you know, we invited you to have your exhibition here
for the winter months as we had declining visitation in
this period during the last two years. This year we are
pleased that we have had over 116,500 visitors during the
period of your exhibition. This has set a record for this
period! We know that several families and individuals came
back four and five times to see the exhibition. The enthusiasm of the visitors was also felt by the staff who have
already expressed their sorrow in not having the creatures
around the building.

We greatly appreciate your involvement in the gallery on
several occasions. Your ability to communicate with our
visitors about the sculpture and your presence added to
the success of the exhibition.

We certainly hope that we will be able to finalize the
acquisition of your Brontosaurus for our museum. We know
that it will be very beneficial to our image and to our
public to have the sculpture here permanently.

Thank you again for the pleasure of having your sculpture
at our museum and for the joy it brought to our staff and
to our visitors.

Sincerely,

Mullie Compton

Mildred S. Compton
Executive Director

MSC:jh

FOUNDED IN 1812
RESEARCH · MUSEUM · EDUCATION

PHILADELPHIA

August 30, 1984

Mr. Jim Gary
P.O. Box 102
Red Bank, NJ 07701

Dear Jim:

It was such a nice surprise to see you the other day and have an
opportunity to show you around the Academy. I especially enjoyed
hearing about your latest works and exhibit openings as well as
sharing our plans and progress on DISCOVERING DINOSAURS. As I no
doubt mentioned to you, this is the most ambitious exhibition the
Academy has ever undertaken and all of us are extremely excited
about its potentially positive impact for the museum.

As we progress on DISCOVERING DINOSAURS, I often think of you and
your first museum exhibition at the Academy five years ago. As
you remember, we were in the middle of a major building
renovation program and giving thought to the future of the
museum, its exhibits and attendance levels. One of our
strategies at that time for increasing our attendance levels was
to have an active changing exhibits program. In fact, your
exhibition of dinosaurs was our first effort towards that
strategy.

I think you'll agree that we both learned many things from that
exhibition. For the Academy, your exhibit not only reinforced
our thoughts concerning the importance of a changing exhibits
program, but more importantly, it dramatically illustrated the
public's thirst for dinosaurs. Your exhibit made us realize that
we had to return dinosaurs to the Academy and Philadelphia in
order to have the attendance levels and public support which we
wanted. In many ways, your exhibition at the Academy was a
catalyst for starting DISCOVERING DINOSAURS and was an
inspiration for including a theme on "art and dinosaurs" as a
part of DISCOVERING DINOSAURS. For you, I can only hope that the
Academy provided some insights into museum exhibition and helped
pave the way for other museum exhibitions. Together, we have
experienced the joys of bringing dinosaurs to life in the
imaginations of the public.

Until your next visit, I wish you continued success and look
forward to working with you in the future. I remain,

Cordially,

Russell S. Daws

Russell S. Daws
Director of Education

THE ACADEMY OF NATURAL SCIENCES OF PHILADELPHIA · 19TH & THE PARKWAY, LOGAN SQUARE · PHILADELPHIA, PA. 19103

4301 McClellan Blvd.   P. O. Box 1587   Anniston, Alabama 36202   Phone 205/237-6766

ANNISTON MUSEUM OF NATURAL HISTORY

February 14, 1985

Mr. Jim Gary
8 Broad Street
Red Bank, NJ 07701

Dear Jim,

On behalf of the Board of Directors and staff of the Anniston Museum of Natural History, I would like to thank you for sharing your wonderful sculptures with our community through your recent exhibit. The exhibition was a great success and will long be remembered by our visitors.

Attendance during the exhibit "Twentieth Century Dinosaurs" September 15 through October 21, 1984 totalled 8,751. This compared to a total of 4,130 visitors during the same 5 week period in 1983. This included visitors to the museum and participants in the numerous special programs associated with the display. The dinosaurs story hour for preschoolers was especially popular, as well as the dinosaur mask and puppetry workshops.

"Twentieth Century Dinosaurs" was also beneficial to the museum in that it marked the first temporary exhibit which attracted sponsorship funding from a local business. We expect that this will set the pattern for future business support of our changing exhibits schedule. The exhibit also received major grant support from the Alabama Bureau of Tourism and Travel which has helped to improve the museum's image as a major tourist attraction for the state. Press coverage of the exhibit was very satisfying and included features in most major newspapers in the area as well as "USA Today."

As you know, it is often difficult for natural history museums to find traveling exhibits of high quality. I would highly recommend your work for display in other institutions and wish you much success in future years.

Sincerely,

Christopher J. Reich

Christopher J. Reich
Director

CJR/ww

MEMBER OF THE AMERICAN ASSOCIATION OF MUSEUMS

The Bruce Museum

October 23, 1979

Mr. Jim Gary
8 Broad Street
Redbank, New Jersey 07701

Dear Jim:

I want to express the appreciation of our Board, staff and exhibit sponsors for your wonderful exhibition. Attendance was well above expectations at around 12,000 for the month. More important than the quantity though was the quality of the exhibit and related programs. People have been calling and coming in with great disappointment to find that the sculptures were no longer with us. The impact of your exhibit and the excitement it generated will be with us for a long time to come.

Needless to say we were also pleased with the number of pieces that sold from the exhibition. We are also very pleased with the two pieces the Museum purchased for its own collections. All in all, a most rewarding and fruitful experience.

Lastly, I must comment on the level of professionalism with which the show was handled. We have seldom experienced such an enjoyable and agreeable situation with an artist.

All of us wish you tremendous success in your future exhibitions and hope that you will not hesitate to stop in when passing through.

Sincerely,

John B. Clark

JBC:l.st.g.   John B. Clark
                               Director

Museum Drive, Greenwich, Connecticut 06830   203·869·0376

FRANK MACRI
President

COMMUNICATIONS DESIGN GROUP

September 3, 1985

Mr. Jim Gary
8 Broad Street
Red Bank, New Jersey   07701

Dear Jim:

The numbers of people that viewed your show were astounding. Not only
is it an exciting show but a real crowd pleaser as well. The media
coverage generated from this exhibit was phenomenal due to its' very
unique and visual appeal.

We at Equitable were pleased to show your work and will certainly
consider a return visit.

Sincerely,

Frank Macri, President
Communications Design Group

P.S. Jim, congratulations on your making the 1985 edition of The New
World Book of Knowledge.

135 WEST 50TH STREET, NEW YORK, NY 10020
A DIVISION OF THE EQUITABLE

St. Louis Science Center

5050 Oakland Avenue
St. Louis, Missouri 63110
(314) 289-4400

July 10, 1986

Mr. Jim Gary
P.O. Box 102
Red Bank, N.J. 07701

Dear Jim:

What a treat it was for the Science Center to host your 20th Century
Dinosaurs from April 3 until July 6 this year! Our attendance
during the exhibit totaled 205,582 enthusiastic children and adults.

The comments ranged from "What fun!" to "the creatures seemed so
life-like and graceful" to "they look like real skeletons!" The
exhibition was a real plus for us and helped us achieve a very
positive image during the first year of the Science Center.

My staff all speak highly of you and of the very good public demonstrations
which you gave on the weekends you were here. The raffle for your
Big Bird for the June 28 Dance-O-Saurus was successful, and I know
the winner - John McDonnell - is very happy to have won.

I am pleased that you liked the signage and labels which could
be used by you again. I feel all our accounts are straight with
you although we still have the freight bill back to New Jersey
to pay.

It was very good to see you again and I hope we can acquire one
of your creations for permanent display.

Best wishes for more successful exhibitions.

Very truly yours,

Dwight S. Crandell
Executive Director

DSC:ws

**MEMPHIS
IS FUN**

MEMPHIS PINK PALACE MUSEUM
Operated by the Memphis Park Commission

3050 CENTRAL AVENUE
MEMPHIS, TN 38111
(901) 454-5603

April 23, 1982

Mr. Jim Gary
Iron Butterfly Studio
8 Broad St.
Red Bank, NJ   07701

Dear Jim:

Forgive the delay in writing to thank you for the outstanding job
you did in seeing not only that the 20th Century Dinosaur Exhibit
was quickly assembled and disassembled but especially for your
superb public relations job on various talk shows and with the
public. 20th Century Dinosaur is remarkable by its ability to
capture the imagination of adults and children wherever it is on
view. You will be interested that attendance for March, which
was the second month for your dinosaurs and also had the four day
display of the Magna Carta, was 43,991 and consequently, the best
month in the 53 year history of the Memphis Pink Palace Museum!

It is enormously difficult for history/natural history museums to
obtain high-quality, three dimensional, traveling exhibits.
Although 20th Century Dinosaurs is not a natural history exhibit
in the strictest sense, it is one of the finest traveling
displays I have seen in my ten years as a museum director. Any
museum with an adequate marketing plan and promotion will
captivate the imagination of the its entire community and can
fully expect the same success we experienced.

It was a great pleasure to get to know you personally and I hope
you realize that you will always be warmly welcomed here.

Sincerely yours,

Douglas R. Noble
Director of Museums

brs

California Academy of Sciences

Natural History
Museum
& Aquarium

16 July 1985

Mr. Jim Gary
P.O. Box 102
Red Bank, New Jersey 07701

Dear Jim:

    Well, DinoFest '85 is off to a good start with fine and happy
attendance. The attached memo from Pam gives you an idea, and it
hasn't stopped since. That should assure a successful summer for
us.

    The Chinese dinosaur has finally arrived so it is being re-
created in Cowell Hall.

    Since plans are moving ahead on the Dino Ball for October 24th,
it would help us to know which sculpture you will give for that
event. In exchange we plan to pay round-trip plane and hotel expenses
for you and Phyllis to attend the Ball. Payment for your last trip
out here is in process.

    Hope your stay here was, as exciting for you as your sculpture is
for us.

    Sincerely,

    Eugene F. Behlen
    Director of Public Programs

EFB:crp
Enclosure

Golden Gate Park   San Francisco, California 94118   (415) 221-5100

*California Academy
of Sciences*

July 10, 1985

Attendance at the first four days of DinoFest '85 totaled 30,977
visitors.

Of that total, 23,950 were paid; 7,027 were free.

This averages 7,744 visitors per day.

This compares to last year, same four days, of a total of 23,310,
representing 17,108 paid, and 6,202 free.

The first four days of the penguin tank opening totals (June 26)
were 17,672, representing 13,407 paid and 4,265 free.

Pam Wing

*Golden Gate Park
San Francisco, California 94118
(415) 221-5100*

California Academy of Sciences

Office of the Director

September 24, 1985

Ms. Phyllis Steigelman
17 Church St.
Middletown, NJ 07748

Dear Phyllis and Jim:

　　I just want to give you a report of the success of the
"Detroit Dinosaurs" which we have turned into Dinofest '85 by
adding childrens activities and some of our own dinosaur material.
The show has been an unqualified success. We had expected a drop
in attendance for July and August as we increased our attendance
fee by 50%. This would have been normally about 10%, but, in fact,
we increased attendance and had an extremely full two months, drawing
over 370,000 people. Our July free day yielded the largest number
of visitors the Academy has ever had (16,700).

　　We have enjoyed the whimsey of the dinosaurs and their
remarkable accuracy, and so have our visitors. I will look
forward to seeing you both on the "Night of the Dinosaurs".

With regards,

Frank H. Talbot

FHT/a

Golden Gate Park　　San Francisco, California 94118　　(415) 221-5100

"We estimate that 212,000 people saw your work" President-FLORIDA A&M

Florida Agricultural and Mechanical University
Tallahassee, Florida
ZIP CODE: 32307

OFFICE OF THE PRESIDENT

August 10, 1978

Mr. Jim Gary
8 Broad Street
Red Bank, New Jersey 07701

Dear Jim:

Floridians are still talking about "Jim Gary and his Creaturations." Without a doubt, Jim, your exhibition during my Inauguration Weekend was one of the most creative and popular artistic acts ever to hit the City of Tallahassee.

We estimate that 212,000 people saw your work, both on-site and via television shows aired in four Florida cities. Approximately 6,000 of these people--including alumni, community citizens, faculty, staff and students--saw your work on display in the Grand Ballroom on campus.

Chester Williams, the art professor who worked so closely with you, tells me that about 500 art students attended your lecture sessions. You probably remember the many thoughtful questions and comments made by our students from sculpture, art design, art appreciation and art education classes.

Jim, I was also very pleased with the turnout of about 2,500 persons for the receptions held at our home and in the Grand Ballroom. I was especially happy for the enthusiastic response to you and your work.

Bob Allen, our director of University Relations, reports that 10,000 viewers watched you and your creaturations on the University's television show, "FAMU Facts & Faces," aired on ABC affiliate WECA-TV in Tallahassee. Another 20,000 saw you on a 90-minute "Inauguration Special" produced by WFSU-TV and aired in Tallahassee, Tampa, Miami and Pensacola.

Appearances by you on evening and night TV news shows on WECA and CBS affiliate WCTV-TV reached an additional 173,000 people.

I have had hundreds of people congratulate me for the strong humanities and fine arts theme prevalent throughout the Inauguration Weekend. Jim, our attempt to present a program of this kind would not have succeeded without a featured quality production such as "Creaturations." It was truly an entertaining, informative and educational experience for all of us.

In behalf of the entire University community, I thank you and wish you well as you continue your work.

Yours truly,

Walter L. Smith

WLS/bwa

"It was truly an entertaining, informative and educational experience for all of us."

May 18, 1983

Mr. Jim Gary
8 Broad Street
Red Bank, New Jersey 07701

Dear Mr. Gary:

Just as a follow-up I would like to express the appreciation and enthusiasm of the Los Angeles County Museum of Natural History for the recent exhibition "20th Century Dinosaurs" which you created and which was on display in the Museum from January 28 to May 1, 1983.

The exhibit created a great deal of exposure for the Museum as it was featured in numerous newspaper stories as well as radio and television spots throughout the Los Angeles area. It was a very attractive show and the media obviously delighted in running stories about it. This was also evidenced by the response from the general public. The Museum attendance during the exhibit was 395,461, an increase of 114,047 over the same period of the previous year. I believe that in itself speaks for the popularity of the show. It certainly proved to be one of if not the most popular special exhibit we have ever had in this Museum and our Director, Dr. Craig C. Black, was personally very pleased with its popularity and response from the public.

As I believe I mentioned earlier, the Museum budgeted $40,000 for the exhibit which included all related costs as well as the rental fee. While the books have not yet been closed, it appears that we will be coming in a little under budget.

Finally, you will be pleased to know that the decision by Dr. Black to keep four of your pieces here for display on our north entrance promenade until the end of August has met with very favorable reaction from both the staff and the visiting public.

Again, on behalf of the Museum of Natural History and thousands of people who viewed your exhibit, I want to express our collective appreciation for your artistic talents and for being able to have your exhibit at our Museum.

Warmest personal regards,

Leon G. Arnold
Assistant Director

LGA:brs

Craig C. Black, *Director*
Leon G. Arnold, *Assistant Director*

NATURAL HISTORY MUSEUM LOS ANGELES COUNTY

Los Angeles County Museum of Natural History • 900 Exposition Boulevard • Los Angeles, California 90007 • tel (213) 744-3414
George C. Page Museum • Hancock Park • 5801 Wilshire Boulevard • Los Angeles, California 90036 • tel (213) 933-7451

Bell Laboratories

Holmdel, New Jersey 07733
Phone (201) 949-3000

December 31, 1981

Mr. James Gary
Iron Butterfly
Eight Broad Street
Red Bank, NJ 07701

Dear Jim:

When we look back at the 1981 cultural exhibits at Holmdel,
your "Twentieth Century Exhibit" was most gratifying.
Our two (2) evenings of open house drew more than 3,000
employees and their families who expressed excitement and
support for your work.

During the four week show, we had a number of visitors who
also reviewed your exhibit. I have attached a list of
those visitors. Also included are photographs of the
show.

We appreciate your sharing your creativity, style and
dedication to the arts and look forward to another exhibit
on your latest accomplishments.

Sincerely,

R. J. Goodall
Supervisor

Milwaukee Public Museum

800 W. Wells St. Milwaukee, WI 53233   414/278-2702

Natural and human history

April 2, 1985

Mr. Jim Gary
Iron Butterfly Studio
8 Broad Street
Red Bank, NJ 07701

Dear Jim:

I hear that your marvelous 20th Century Dinosaurs are still burning up excitement
whereever they go. They are still talked about around the Museum, and by
Milwaukeeans who had an opportunity to catch them while they were displayed
at the Museum. Several people who were unable to see them, but heard about the
display after it was gone were very disappointed not to have had the chance to
see these spectacular creations.

I am enclosing some of your slides and pictures that were recently discovered
during a cleanup by one of the television interviewers you saw. I hope their
unavailability did not overly inconvenience you.

You may be interested to know that there have been some changes in operation
around here since your visit. Some things, albeit not enough, are being
tightened up, and some people made accountable. I hope you're not discouraged
from stopping in should you get back this way again.

Much continued success developing and expanding your artform. I'll always
remember their hulking charm.

Sincerely,

Norma J. Balentine
Asst. Public Affairs Officer

Enclosure

An educational and cultural resource of Milwaukee County

FIELD MUSEUM
OF NATURAL HISTORY

October 30, 1984

Jim Gary
P. O. Box 102
Red Banks, New Jersey 07701

Dear Jim:

On behalf of Field Museum of Natural History, I want to thank you for your delightful exhibit of 20th Century Dinosaurs. They were a great addition to our annual Dinosaur Days celebration and certainly captured the imagination of everyone who saw them. Their presence in Stanley Field Hall created considerable enthusiasm among the museum staff too. Even the scientific staff were impressed with them. As you can see from the enclosed photographs from the two major Chicago newspapers, they were a great hit throughout Chicago.

We all enjoyed getting to know you. Hopefully, we can have you back soon again. Good luck to you in the future and keep in touch.

Sincerely,

Susan E. Stob
Head, Public Programs
Department of Education

SES:vsr

Ms. Gunther's footnotes and bibliography:

[1] Hilton Kramer, *The Age of the Avant-Garde,* Farrar, Straus and Giroux (New York, 1973), p. 397.

[2] Jack Burnham, *Beyond Modern Sculpture,* George Braziller, Inc. (New York, 1967), p. 19.

[3] *Ibid.*

[4] *Ibid.*

[5] *Ibid.,* p. 20.

[6] Kramer, *op. cit.,* p. 399.

[7] *Ibid.*

[8] *Ibid.*

[9] *Ibid.*

[10] *Ibid.,* p. 396.

[11] Burnham, *op. cit.,* p. 245.

[12] *Ibid.*

[13] *Ibid.*

[14] H.J. Scheepmaker, ed., *Adventure in Art,* Harry N. Abrams, Inc. (New York, 1969), p. 150.

[15] Kramer, *op. cit.,* p. 453.

[16] *Ibid.*

[17] Douglas Davis, *Art and the Future,* Praeger Publishers (New York, 1973), p. 62.

[18] *Ibid.,* p. 40.

Burnham, Jack, *Beyond Modern Sculpture,* New York: George Braziller, Inc., 1967.

Davis, Douglas, *Art and the Future,* New York: Praeger Publishers, 1973.

Kramer, Hilton, *The Age of the Avant-Garde,* New York: Farrar, Straus and Giroux, 1973.

Scheepmaker, H.J., ed., *Adventure in Art,* New York: Harry N. Abrams, Inc., 1969.

Photo Credits

Frontispiece: "Dragonslayer" by Jim Gary at the Los Angeles County Museum of Natural History.

Page iv—Tova Navarra.

3. A scene from George Lucas' film "Howard the Duck" with a Jim Gary Stegosaurus. Courtesy of Universal Pictures.

4. Left, Susan Rosenberg; top & lower right, Tova Navarra.

5. Captain Kangaroo (Bob Keeshan) and Jim Gary. Susan Rosenberg.

7. "Universal Woman" by Jim Gary. Tova Navarra.

12., 13., 19., 20., 21., 23., 28., 29., 36., 37., 38., 46., 60., 63. Courtesy of Jim Gary.

16. Tova Navarra.

18. Susan Rosenberg.

25. Jeff Lega

26. "Signs of the Times" by Jim Gary. Courtesy of the artist.

27. *The Sunday Register,* Red Bank

30. Baptismal Font by Jim Gary, made for St. Benedict's Church, Holmdel Township, N.J.

32. Jeff Lega

33. Susan Rosenberg.

34., 35. Tova Navarra.

39. Top, Courtesy of Jim Gary; bottom, Jim Gary with driver Bryan Culberston. Tova Navarra.

40. Crew of "Ripley's Believe It or Not!" creating footage of Gary at his Hightstown, N.J., shop. Tova Navarra.

41. The Ripley's film crew at Boston Museum of Sciences. Tova Navarra.

42. Left to right: Bryan Gary, Gretchen Gary, Jim Gary the artist, Andrew Gary and James R. Gary; "Carburetor Person" by Jim Gary. Tova Navarra.

43, 45. Tables by Jim Gary. Courtesy of the artist.

47. "Allosaurus" by Jim Gary. Tova Navarra.

48. Tova Navarra; "Ankylosaurus," and "Spring Neck Bird" by Jim Gary.

49. "XAX." Courtesy of the artist.

50. Menorah made for the Jewish Community Center, Howell Township; "Brass Bitch" by Jim Gary.

51. Painting the "Eryops" and welding. Tova Navarra.

53. "Howard the Duck" cards. © Marvel Comics Group 1986.

54. Glen Campbell with Jim Gary. Courtesy of the artist.

55. Top, Tova Navarra; bottom, Courtesy of the artist.

56. "Spring Neck Bird" by Jim Gary. Susan Rosenberg.

57. "Tree." Richard Tashjian.

61. Arlene Berg.

67. "Torso with Flower." Tova Navarra.

68. "Alligator." Courtesy of the artist.

69. *Geo* magazine cover. Courtesy of the National Geographic Society.

78. "Dimetrodon." Courtesy of *Welding Journal.*

79. Courtesy of *N.J. Music & Arts* magazine.

80. Courtesy of the Los Angeles County Museum of Natural History.

81. "Stained Glass Lady." Tova Navarra.

83. Head of a Bird by Jim Gary. Courtesy of the artist.

About the Author

Tova Navarra's fondness for the sculpture of Jim Gary began when Louis de Furia, then publisher of New Jersey Music & Arts magazine, introduced her to his longtime favorite who needed a writer and publicist. De Furia thought Ms. Navarra, a *magna cum laude* graduate of Seton Hall University's art and music department, full-time art and music teacher at Seton Hall Preparatory School and staff writer for Music & Arts, would write about Gary's work with enthusiasm and understanding.

Ms. Navarra had noticed but not spoken to Gary years before, however, when she and Gary were participants in art shows in Atlantic City and elsewhere. As Gary moved into museum exhibitions, Ms. Navarra went on to illustrate *Drugs and Man* (Doubleday & Co., 1973), and contribute illustrations to other publications. She left teaching to become a stringer at the Asbury Park Press, where she is now a full-time reporter.

Her book *The New Jersey Shore: A Vanishing Splendor,* published by the Philadelphia Art Alliance & Associated University Presses in October 1985, is a text and a collection of photographs Ms. Navarra had taken from 1979 through 1981 as founder, publisher and editor of Shore Affinity, a monthly tabloid.

She is also the author of *Dog Star* (1987) and a contributing illustrator of *Song of Songs,* to be published by Golden Cockerel Press, London. Her photographs of Gary's sculpture have appeared in *The Book of Knowledge Annual* (Grolier, Inc., 1985), the Asbury Park Press, *Running Free* (Scott, Foresman & Co., 1987), USA Today, and in many newspapers and magazines throughout the United States.

In addition to her artistic endeavors, Ms. Navarra is a graduate of Brookdale Community College nursing program and a registered nurse. She has worked as a charge nurse in a psychiatric facility, and often writes health-related articles for the Asbury Park Press and *RN* and *Today's OR Nurse* magazines.

Ms. Navarra's husband, John Gabriel Navarra, Jr., is a N.J. attorney and a physics teacher at Christian Brothers Academy. They reside in Monmouth County with their two children, Yolanda, an Asbury Park Press staff writer, and John III, an aspiring musician.

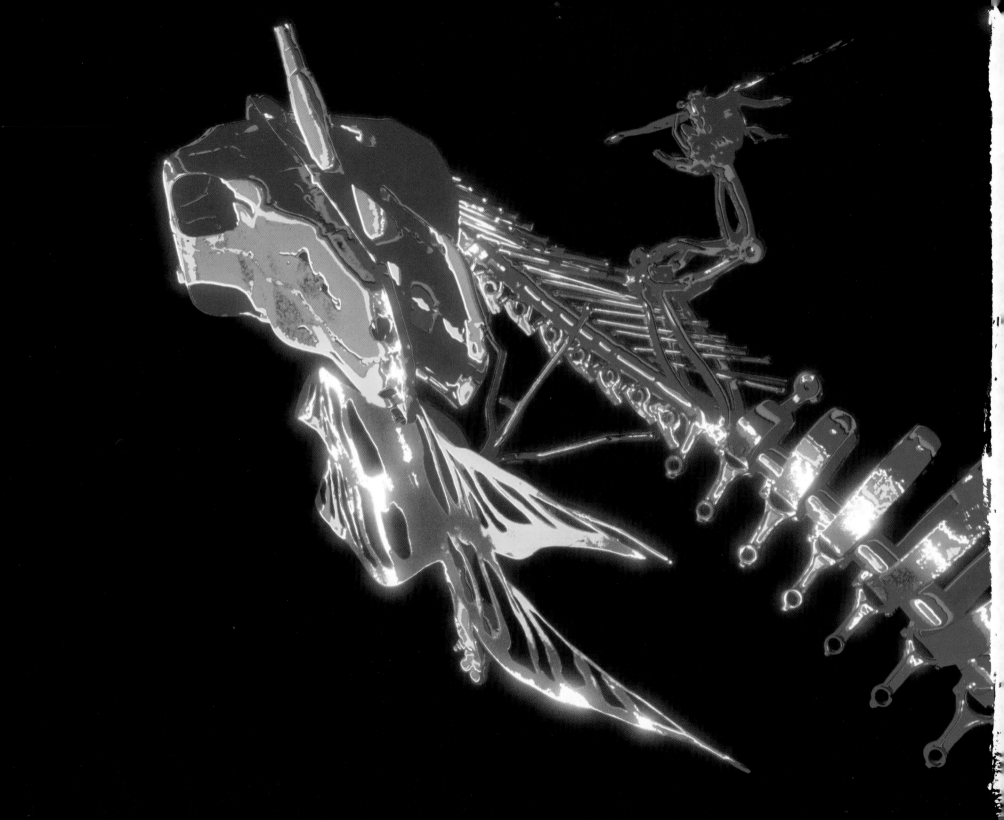